SUDDENLY SINGLE

Suddenly Single

PHIL STANTON

KINGSWAY PUBLICATIONS
EASTBOURNE

ISBN 0 85476 645 6

Designed and produced by
Bookprint Creative Services
P.O. Box 827, BN21 3YJ, England for
KINGSWAY PUBLICATIONS LTD
Lottbridge Drove, Eastbourne, E. Sussex BN23 6NT.
Printed in Great Britain.

To B,
whose initiative and encouragement
proved invaluable.

Contents

Introduction

What I've written about I've lived through myself, although I have suppressed the personal details that would be an embarrassment to my family. Sadly, there is nothing unique nowadays about somebody's partner leaving. Many are suffering, many are yet to suffer.

As a minister of the word of God, I had always tried to help the suddenly single, but it wasn't until I became suddenly single myself that I realised I had never really understood them. I wished I could go back and start afresh with them. So much is written, taught and known about courtship and God's pattern for married life, but when it comes to sudden singlehood there seems to be a huge gap.

I received this letter some while ago:

When my husband left me, I felt as if I were stranded in the middle of a desert without a map, lonely and lost. I believed the Bible, but couldn't find the answers for my present situation. I searched in Christian bookshops for biblical books on the subject, but to no avail. I suppose many Christians, like myself, don't know where to look in the Bible for guidance in these heartbreaking circumstances.

I was very sorry to hear about your wife leaving you. But knowing your understanding of the Bible, I hope that you will use all that pain to write a book, to help others whose partners leave them.

There appears to be a real need for teaching from the word of God on coping with sudden singlehood, so I have written for all sufferers, male and female – and their counsellors – in the name of him who is 'a strength to the poor, a strength to the needy in his distress, a refuge from the storm, a shade from the heat; for the blast of the terrible ones is as a storm against the wall' (Is 25:4).

1
Suddenly Single

The forsaken husband's story

Suddenly she is gone. Now you are single. You had no idea there was someone else. She *had* been behaving rather strangely of late, but there was no reason to think that anything was wrong. Not *seriously* wrong.

But it was you who was wrong. She has found someone else, and she loves him. You are to be left alone, with no one to hug, touch, confide in or love. It is no good pleading; there are no arguments that make any difference. She has everything planned, and she is going.

But you plead anyway. Surely some appeal will touch her. If logic and good sense will not do, then perhaps tears will. Your tears come very easily. Can't she see how much you love her? You would do anything, *anything*, if only she would stay. It seems that she has not been happy. She says she has never been happy. Is this really so? No matter, because you will change – change so radically that she is bound to be happy. No change will be too great. In these last minutes you've already begun the change. If she could just tell you – all right, tell you again – you'll know what to change. She has told you so many times before? She can't bear to go through it all again? Well, you can understand that. You've been so blind in the past; you don't mind admitting it. But it'll be different in the future.

She doesn't love you any more. In fact, she's not sure that she ever did. Ah, this is much harder. You just need a moment to think about that. In fact, it isn't easy to speak for the moment. But wait, even this mountain can be climbed. You love her enough for two. No good? Well, you'll win her love as never before. She doesn't believe that. Come to think of it, neither do you. After all, you have just discovered that you are unlovable. You had half-suspected it all your life, but now, in just a few moments, you have reached absolute conviction: you are not lovely, not to her, not to anyone. How then can you win her love?

Oh, and by the way, she is taking the children too. And we must talk about how we tell them. Of course it will be difficult for them, but they'll get used to the new arrangement. She wants you to know that you will still see them. They will still need their dad. But all you can see is their little faces when the bombshell falls. You will see something precious destroyed that can never be rebuilt. And then, when you wake in the morning, there won't be those getting-up noises, the flurry of getting ready in time for school. There will just be you.

How could she have betrayed you? You love her, and through these recent weeks, when things seemed a bit different, you tried so hard to show her your love. When she seemed sad, you tried to comfort her. You had no idea that she was sad because she wasn't with *him*. What about the promises, the plans you had made together? What about the years you've had together? She says that she was never happy. But you were happy with her. Does that count for nothing? How could she betray you – and not just you, but your God, your children, your friends, your whole world?

It makes you furious just to think about it. Surely there is nothing so underhand, so dishonest, so despicable, as what she has done. Whatever faults you might have had, you don't deserve this! It's enough to make your blood boil that after all you've done – your love, your sacrifices – she can just go off and do this! If we are talking about marriage, there's one or two points you would like to make. She's not the only one who's been unhappy. The difference is, *you* always forgave, made the best of it and stuck to your vows.

The more you think about it, the more her betrayal appears in all its foul colours. The more you think about it! It's funny how you can't stop thinking about it, going over the same ground in your mind. Perhaps you should stop thinking about it now, just for a while, because you're going to need to eat something sometime. And then there's tonight. If you don't get any sleep you won't be good for anything at all. So you'll stop thinking about it. Soon, you're bound to stop thinking about it.

Perhaps she will change her mind. Perhaps you will both look back at this dreadful time and smile at 'that crazy mood that came over her'. Nothing has been destroyed yet. She will change her mind, you will forgive her, and things will return to normal. God will answer this prayer – this most urgent prayer of your whole life. How can he say 'no'? Really, all of this has been a kind of 'test'. God is watching to see if you will keep believing and praying. The answer is sure to come, and it is bound to be soon. Then, when you're both happy together again, you'll be glad you kept trusting. What a testimony you'll have!

Lord, I'm ready to change. How blind I've been!

Those little things she didn't like about me weren't so little to her. But now, Lord, with your help, I will change, and think how happy she will be! Lord, I receive this new gift of love for her. By your grace, I will become the person she wants me to be. Dear Lord, I'm sorry I took her for granted; help me to be different from now on.

There's something about the way she closed the door behind her just then. She's done it thousands of times before, but never like this. Because this time it means 'goodbye' – not just 'see you later'. From the sound of her footsteps outside, she is moving quickly. There's someone waiting for her – someone she loves – and she can't wait to be with him.

Once she has gone and you are truly alone, a terrible emptiness stretches ahead of you. The numbness and shock soon pass. Not so the loneliness. That has moved in, and plans to stay with you – for ever. Along with loneliness, your new companion, there is a crowd of new thoughts. These thoughts have come to torture you. It is clear now that you were never lovable. There is something fundamentally wrong with you. That's why God has allowed this to happen. That's why she couldn't stay in love with you. Who indeed has ever truly loved you? No one, surely, who knew you as she did.

There is a funny thing about these thoughts: they can never keep still. They insist on going round and round, all the time. Late at night, when you need to sleep, they are active. Early in the morning, long before you should have woken up, there they are, fresh and lively.

It's never occurred to you before, but shouldn't there be some sort of measure for unhappiness? Surely you are now more unhappy than you had ever believed possible.

How unhappy is that? Well past the 'bearable' mark; you know that. The trouble is, there doesn't seem to be any end in sight – not in this life anyway.

It is strange to wonder if you will even survive. That isn't a question that would have occurred to you before. Well, will you? You're not sure. You might die inside. People do, you've heard. They just become dull and drab. They lose that sparkle. They are rather pathetic sights. They absorb sympathy like sponges, but really it's an effort to be with them because they are so, well, grey. There are a few *you* have been sorry for. You never thought you might become like them.

Perhaps you will become bitter and vengeful. You're not sure that this hasn't already happened. And God knows, you have reason enough. She deserves all she gets. But you can't forget that bit about forgiving others as God forgives us. People who won't forgive won't be forgiven. Would this apply in your case? You fear it would, so somehow you must fight this bitterness, because your very life is at stake.

It's been so easy for her – she has her new partner – but what about you? You see, you've been wondering about meeting someone new as well. It's not so much a new wife as a *woman* you're thinking about. It's not love, but sex. She'll see that she isn't the only one who can get someone into bed. But wait – you can't do that, you're a Christian. It's horrifying and shameful just to think these things! How could you have even entertained such thoughts? As a Christian, you will put these thoughts away, and never think them again. Unless you get too lonely, too frustrated. . . .

How easily these thoughts come! If only they would go as easily, because it may be that God is all you have left. And the deepest truth is that you don't *want* to do bad things. But wouldn't it be great to have your own fling just for once! Then she would see that she is not the only one who can play that game. Not that she would ever find out. No one must find out. Except God. Of course, he would be bound to know. And you would know. And really it isn't what you want. Dear God, make this something that I do not want.

Has it shocked you, thinking this way? I mean, such a saintly person like you, entertaining such sordid thoughts? Oh, you didn't say you were a saint? Well, you certainly sound like one. Such a fine, faithful, patient husband, and she such a monster! Has it occurred to you that you've been bolstering yourself up in your thoughts? Or perhaps you really are the wonderful saint you seem, and she has been the monster – cold, hard and loveless – that your thoughts now make her out to be. Maybe you should search your memory. Were *you* ever selfish, unkind, thoughtless? Did you ever take her for granted? Did you really listen, really communicate?

Ah, I see from your face that I've hit the mark. No wait – I understand, I really do understand: anyone, at a time like this, would try to justify themselves. I expect she is doing the same. Just so long as you know you're doing it – that's all I'm saying.

And what about money? It's funny how important such material things are in the midst of your grief. How will you live if the house must be sold and you have to pay a crippling maintenance? Or perhaps you are the one with the children. You will be a single parent, living on a pittance. Can you face the terror and insecurity of it all? Maybe you never dealt with the financial matters. How are you going to run your finances? Already a number of things occur to you that you will no longer be able to afford. Will you be able to have the heating on as you used to? What sort of foods are cheap and yet worth looking forward to? The children keep needing new clothes, new shoes, but surely there won't be a problem finding money for that, will there?

Then there is the issue of other people. Suddenly you're longing for them and dreading seeing them, both at the same time. Now you're single all of a sudden, it's all going to be different. He was such a fun person; now he's sympathetic, embarrassed and clumsy all at the same time. She offers mounds of counsel and advice; you just wish she'd stop and leave you alone. She doesn't know what it's like. He didn't say much, but he said enough: he hinted that it's your fault she left. He didn't exactly say it, but you know what he meant. With friends like this, you won't need enemies. But here's another friend who doesn't say much at all: she just hugs you, and cries a bit, and says how sorry she is. She doesn't know how your soul drinks in the kindness she offers. At least no one is trying to pry, just for curiosity's sake. That would be unbearable.

Isn't it strange how drained you feel after you've seen them all? It was good to be with your friends, but emotionally exhausting too. It's easier, in a way, to be on your own. At least you don't have to make the effort. Your own company is strangely comforting. You make no demands on yourself, you're sympathetic towards your unhappiness, and you try to keep off the really painful ground. There are a few things you couldn't do before, and you treat yourself to these comforting pleasures now. The only thing is, might you become a bit of a recluse?

If only someone really understood you. If only – impossible thought! – someone could love you, now, *today*, as you really are. If only you could be happy again. It doesn't seem as if that will ever be.

The forsaken wife's story

As I kneel by the foot of our bed, I start to pray. Tears stream down my face, and I am almost too exhausted to think.

Lord, forgive me. A few moments ago I was looking in the wardrobe for that special dress. I looked at myself in the mirror, and with each stroke of the brush I heard myself saying: 'I'll show him. I'll show him.' I watched my reflection as I put on my lipstick.

I feel so unloved, unwanted and rejected. Like a ball of waste paper, thrown in the bin. I wanted to show him that I too could find someone – outside our marriage.

'Then he will know,' I said, 'what infidelity feels like.' But looking at my eyes in the mirror, I see that these are the eyes of a Christian, and have been for a long time. I feel so ashamed of what I have been thinking. I realise that I – body and soul – belong to Jesus.

I feel my anger subsiding, but I feel no better. Do you love me, Lord? This present situation seems to contradict your love. Why are you allowing this to happen?

The man who shares this bed with me, the father of my children, my friend, my husband. . . . This man says that *they love one another*. They want to spend the rest of their lives together.

My mind still reels with these awful words. The months of strange, aloof behaviour; suspicions that I wouldn't allow myself to hold; his new coldness. And then the letter. Discovered by accident, it came like a bombshell. And like a bombshell, it destroyed my life.

His letter; to her. What did I expect him to say about

it? There were to be apologies, excuses and explanations, then the solemn reassurance that the affair had been a terrible mistake. He loved the children and me more than he loved her. 'How could I put at risk what I love most?' he was to say. 'I'll never see her again.' And then he would say that we would have a fresh start, if only I would give him another chance.

That was how it was supposed to happen. But nothing was further from his mind. When I faced him with this shameful letter, he had no shame.

There was a dreadful honesty about how much he wanted to be with her. He seemed almost relieved that it was out in the open. He had no reassurances, no promises.

He doesn't love me any more.

Not that he was always so honest. It was all there, in clues and signs, for all but the blindest to see: those unexplained trips, the strangely private phone calls . . . Did he think me such a fool, I wonder? Well, *I* think me such a fool! I was so gullible, so accepting. Some of those explanations! How could I have believed them?

He had lost his taste for church, and I had wondered why. And why did he treat me more like a sister than a wife? Why didn't he need me as he used to?

Ah well, it is all too obvious now. Had all this happened to a friend, I would have seen it. 'It's another woman,' I would have said. How could I have been so trusting? Because I loved him.

Love! 'We love one another,' he says. And, 'It is real love.' He says that I wouldn't understand.

Would not understand *real love*? So what is it that I have given him all these years?

My mind recalls the numerous sacrifices I have made – all the love that I have given – and my self-pity begins turning to bitterness. Who would not be bitter with all that thrown back in their face? Did he ever love me? Have I, then, been living a lie all these years? So why did he marry me? How could he if there was no real love between us?

But he did love me. I cannot have been wrong about that.

Marriage is a lifelong covenant. He knew that. So how could he have married me if he didn't really love me?

Our marriage was to be for ever. Divorce could never happen to us. We are Christians! How could he? How could he . . .?

Dear Lord, please, please don't let me become bitter. I have seen bitterness get a foothold in others and their lights are quenched, their souls consumed; they are destroyed. And I have no wish to be destroyed, because it will also affect the children.

Oh . . . the children! Dear Lord, how am I to tell them? Please give me the words. For, you see, I can picture their little hearts breaking with the anguish. How can I help them understand? But then, dear Father, I don't understand it myself.

With Dad gone, their little worlds will fall apart. And what words can prepare them for that? Our dear son – Daddy is his hero. 'Daddy's little girl' has lost her protection now. There are just no words to sugar *that* pill.

Lord, I dedicate my life to them. But is Mummy enough on her own? Somehow I don't think so. How can I get them through? I'm not sure that I *can* get through without him. I feel so vulnerable without him. He is my life.

Or rather he was. Oh, dear Father, help me! I am setting out on a new life, all alone, and I am terrified.

Telling Mum and Dad was the hardest thing I ever did. I thought Mum was going to faint. The shock was so great, she couldn't say a word at first. It was as if a great oak were felled with one blow. Her face seemed to age a hundred years with the shock.

I felt so bad, Lord, causing her all that pain. It's so unfair for them. The end of my marriage is like a stone flung in the water: the ripples of anguish just keep spreading and spreading. The forsaken wife, the deserted children, the heartbroken parents. It's unfair for me too: I had to be the one to tell them. I had to smash their happiness.

Dad thought of the practical issues. 'What will you do for money?' he asked. I have enough on my plate without that worry, but he's right. What *will* happen to us? Here is another sea of uncertainty that I shall have to navigate. He handled the finances. How much will we need to live on? The truth is, I don't really know. Will we keep the house? Even that is at risk. Are the children going to lose everything? Will I be able to keep my job if I am to be both Mum and Dad?

He had thought of money, and his offers were very generous. But words are cheap. He will have her to look after now; two households instead of one.

I don't feel like facing people. I can't bear all the questions and explanations. Every time I tell someone, I seem to die a little bit more. I stand in the school playground, waiting for the children. I stand bravely, confidently, but inside I am shattered. People pat me on the shoulders and congratulate me on how bright I look. And I tell them that it's because I am a Christian. 'I trust God,' I say. 'He helps me through it.' But the truth is that I don't understand at all. Am I being punished, Lord?

Those playground mothers: they must be much better

than I. Their husbands haven't been taken away. But what have I done? I just don't understand.

Lord, how can so much happen in so short a time? Days pass like years since my life died. As for him, I hardly know him now. He has changed beyond recognition. That gentle man . . . now he is hard and aloof. Those eyes are cold and dead when he looks at me. Is this the Christian man I married? The soul of a stranger has possessed those familiar features.

What plans we had, he and I! Two young Christians, full of love and confidence. We had God, we had each other – what else could we need? I can remember that young excitement, that zest for life, as if it were yesterday. How we loved you, Lord! How I prayed that I might live up to his wonderful example! 'Let me be a Christian like him,' I used to pray. 'Give me his generous spirit.'

And so our marriage would blossom, hand-in-hand with Jesus, ever closer and nearer. But then he changed. How could he? He let go of your hand, Jesus. Then he let go of mine.

Never let me go, Lord. I would rather let go of life. Why can't I die, and you carry me to heaven? Life does not make sense to me any more. It has lost all its attraction. My marriage was my life. I am a mother and wife, and without that I cannot go on.

I love you, Lord. Why can't I be with you? I don't like this world of pain – it's too much for me to bear. I feel so betrayed. I have lost my best friend – and my husband too.

Dear Lord, I wish I could sit on your lap and cry. . . .

Hopeless? Thank God it's not! There is real hope, for real people such as you and me. God's word comes to us, not with glib platitudes, but with real solutions. There are promises you can take hold of which will prove firm as mountains. There is a solid rock to stand on, and however fearful the storm, you will be standing when all is done.

These promises are for 'Him' and 'Her', without distinction, so I make no further distinction. I have given the partner who left a name – 'Lee'. I have no real-life 'Lee' in mind, but it's a name that could apply equally as well to a man or a woman. Imagine it's the name of your departed partner, and read what follows as written specifically for you.

2

Betrayed!

Let's talk about how it feels to be betrayed. You feel that your love betrayed you. In what ways? Come on, it's good to verbalise how you feel about it. OK, we both know that there's another side to it, that Lee has a right to put forward a case, but we're just talking about you at the moment. Do you want to go through life feeling betrayed? No? Well then.

Don't think that I'm coming to you with easy answers. The truth *is* simple, but finding it is anything but. Any 'simple' answers that I had were swept away in my own devastation, so I searched the Scriptures for true answers; not 'professionally', as a Bible teacher, but because I wanted to survive. 'My soul melts from heaviness; strengthen me according to Your word' (Ps 119:28). All this has been searched out in the Scriptures and hammered out on the anvil of experience, in the red-hot fire of misery.

But first things first. Tell me how you feel. So your love left you. Lee betrayed the marriage vows, but there is more to it than that. There were so many intimate moments, so many special secrets between you, and these were like a thousand extra marriage vows, reinforcing your oneness. There were the special names you

24

had for each other; the jokes only you two understood.

Then there are the memories. What a lot of memories there are! Good memories, I mean. Memories that can never be repeated: moving into a first house; holding a first child in your arms. You shared moments of weakness, when you comforted each other and gave each other strength. You've said things to each other which you could never have said to anyone else.

You've known such joys and sorrows together, and now Lee has betrayed it all by leaving. Worse still, Lee is sharing these things with someone else. How could they? Does Lee use the same pet names? Do they share the same private jokes? How could they?

But it's not just the marriage that has been betrayed. You feel the betrayal has affected everything. What about the children? How could Lee have wrenched their world apart? There was an unspoken vow to them: the family will always stick together. And what about God? Didn't the two of you share a faith in him? And all this has been a shock, a terrible blow, to others too. Your friends in the church, in fact all your friends, are shaken. Perhaps there are younger folk who looked up to you both, who wanted to be a bit like you: they've been betrayed.

How has all this affected your house, your money? Don't you feel betrayed by all the alarming changes there? In fact, don't you feel betrayed almost all the time – deep down, I mean? Seeing some familiar thing; missing something you once had; being alone; remembering. . . .

Since we are being honest, let me ask you: Do you feel that God has betrayed you? Maybe you believe it is wrong to blame God for things. So do I, but that doesn't mean I haven't done it. Perhaps you're thinking: 'I trusted that God would look after my life. I trusted him for my marriage. I prayed for things, and God answered me, but when it really mattered, where was he?'

Have you wondered whether he, like Lee, could just stop loving you? Maybe if he did you couldn't blame him. You wonder if you are worth loving anyway. Some people feel like that. I did. I couldn't see how all this pain fitted in with God loving me. I resented his betrayal, but felt so unlovely that I couldn't really blame him either.

Maybe you feel like this, and perhaps you're ashamed that you do. But listen, God has something to say.

What does the Bible say?

Is God changeable? Does he love people and then go off them? Does he suddenly realise what we are really like, and then ditch us? No. If we really knew what he has already done for us – and how long he has been doing it – we could never feel betrayed by him.

Let's look at what God has done. How long have you loved him? However long it is, it is nowhere near as long as he has loved you. God 'chose us in Him [Christ] before the foundation of the world, that we should be holy and without blame before Him in love' (Eph 1:4). How wonderful to be 'holy and without blame' before God! To be purified like that, we must be saved from all sin. How much God loves us, to do that! But, even more, 'He chose us' for that. When you love someone, you will choose them rather than the others. How God must love us, to do that for us! And then notice that this happened 'before the foundation of the world', long before we had done anything that might have earned this love. Sometimes we feel that we have to be specially nice, or bring a present, so that people will like us. But

26

God's love for us is so enormous! It was fixed on us long before we could do that.

That's how the Lord can say to us: 'I have loved you with an *everlasting* love; therefore with lovingkindness I have drawn you' (Jer 31:3, italics mine). His love for us was not some new thing. He didn't begin to be interested in us when we became interested in him, and he didn't even begin when we came into existence at conception. He had already loved us for longer than we can imagine. When we began to seek him, it was because 'with lovingkindness I have drawn you'.

We mustn't think that this is just some general sort of love. It is not an overall love for vast numbers of people, among whom we might be overlooked. God's love is intensely personal. Jesus said: 'I am the good shepherd' (Jn 10:11), and the shepherd in the Bible didn't use sheepdogs. He had a personal knowledge of his sheep. 'I know My sheep,' says Jesus (v. 14). What does he mean by 'know'? In the next verse he says: 'As the Father knows Me, even so I know the Father.' The Father and the Son know each other with great intimacy and love.

Jesus doesn't need to pile up impressive descriptions of his love. He proves it in action: 'The good shepherd gives His life for the sheep' (v. 11). Notice that he *gives* his life – 'No one takes it from Me, but I lay it down of Myself' (v. 18). Now what sort of love is that? The Father's love for us is just the same. 'Therefore My Father loves Me, because I lay down My life' (v. 17). How could the Father be glad at Jesus' death? Only if he loved us so much that he entirely willed Jesus' dreadful death for us.

But perhaps we have to earn this love, and if we fall beneath the standard we will stop being his sheep. No and no. Jesus tells us how we became his sheep. We became Jesus' sheep because the Father gave us to him:

27

'My Father, who has given them to Me, is greater than all' (v. 29). What about faith? What about our giving ourselves to Jesus? We believe and follow Jesus because we are, 'from before the foundation of the world', his sheep. To those who rejected him, he said: 'You do not believe, because you are not of My sheep' (v. 26). We, who tend to think of earning or deserving love, would put it the other way round. 'Because you don't believe,' we would say, 'you aren't one of his sheep.' We naturally think of *our* doing and believing as the decisive things. But Jesus' words say something different. The Father gave us to Jesus. From then on, he counted us as his sheep. And then, in due course, he gives us faith, and we begin to trust him. Faith itself is 'the gift of God' (Eph 2:8). Because we are his sheep we believe.

This is unconditional love. This is being loved in spite of all the good reasons why we shouldn't be loved. This is unspeakably comforting, and it is true.

I came to believe these things many years ago. Before that, I didn't want to believe that we are 'chosen' – it seemed to make life predictable, predestined. I think I was compelled to accept this rather like John in C.S. Lewis' *The Pilgrim's Regress*.[1] There is a powerful picture in that of the hero, John, drawing closer to faith in Christ. He is on a narrow path dug out of the side of a mountain, going where truth seems to lead. Then he realises, to his horror, that he is being led towards Christ – not what he wants at all! He turns to retreat, and is met by 'Reason', a stern swordswoman, clad in full armour. 'Back! Do you want to fight?' she says.

---

[1] C.S. Lewis, *The Pilgrim's Regress* (Fount Books 1933), pp.210–211.

It was the same with me. Having believed the Bible, I couldn't turn back from the conclusion that true believers are chosen, predestined by God. We were loved before we did anything good. I could fight no longer, but once I surrendered, defeat was sweet. I tried my best, as before, to trust and obey; perhaps now I tried harder. I knew it was up to me to follow Christ, but something new had come: unconditional love. *Because* he has loved me from before the foundation of the world – because he chose me – I want to please him. And I feel secure, because I know that he will never betray me.

Once I understood these things, a great load fell off my back. It was such a relief to know that my security was entirely in God. And I felt that I fully understood these truths. But that was before the disaster. When the blow fell, everything was in turmoil. But out of that turmoil I found that I believed these truths more, and felt more of the power of them. They had come through the holocaust unscathed and strengthened.

So however strange this seems to you, you need to know now more than ever how much God loves you. You need to know that his is an unconditional love. So look again at these words of Jesus – and believe!

Let us stop and think of how great God's love is for us. It is older than the world; it is strong enough to die for; it is close, personal and intimate; it is entirely unearned. And it will never end. Do you really think that after all that has happened to you God will stop loving you? Well, he won't. 'I give them eternal life, and they shall never perish; neither shall anyone snatch them out of My hand' (Jn 10:28). To his true sheep here is wonderful security.

Why then did he let this happen? We'll talk about that in the next chapter, but you can be sure of this: he still loved you when he let it happen. He loves you now.

Becoming suddenly single is a time of dreadful turmoil. It is as if you have lived your life in the quiet centre of a tornado, and then suddenly the storm which you never thought existed is upon you. The cataclysm is reckless and destructive, so to ask: 'Do you feel that God is close to you?' seems a little inappropriate. I felt that God was both very close and a million miles away at the same time. I felt that I was seeking him and relinquishing him simultaneously. Not everyone would understand this, but *you* probably will. Perhaps you feel the same.

In any case, reach out in response to his everlasting love now – even though you may hardly feel it. Maybe this would be a good time to put down this book and pray. He knows you need him more than ever. 'Draw near to God and He will draw near to you' (Jas 4:8). Don't let feeling wretched deter you. 'I found trouble and sorrow. Then I called upon the name of the Lord; O Lord, I implore You, deliver my soul! Gracious is the Lord, and righteous; yes, our God is merciful. The Lord preserves the simple; I was brought low, and He saved me' (Ps 116:3–6).

God loves us so much. He knows that we don't feel our need of him so much in the good times. But he is so good. Now that you've found trouble and sorrow, you'll find him there for you. You'll find him 'gracious and merciful'. Don't hold back.

Jesus understands betrayal

When we cry out to Jesus, it's good to remember that he understands. As God, he understands all things, but also, as man, he has studied betrayal in the School of Life. If they give out PhDs there, he has one. When his time of crisis came, he had a group of special friends, his apostles, with whom he had lived and worked for three years. They had shared a whole range of experiences: miracles, glory and popularity, as well as hunger, opposition and danger. They had come to see that Jesus is the Christ, the Saviour the Old Testament promised. During those years Jesus had needed to put them right time and again, but it was nothing compared with the final hours. It must have seemed to Jesus like one long betrayal.

Jesus made it clear that the Last Supper was very special to him: 'With fervent desire I have desired to eat this Passover with you before I suffer' (Lk 22:15). Surely that would have put his friends on their best behaviour; made them think, 'If this is special to Jesus, let's make sure he enjoys it.' But no, we find 'a dispute among them, as to which of them should be considered the greatest' (v. 24). Jesus had to sort it out, and repeat what he had said in the past about humility and servanthood.

Then he told Peter that he was praying for him, because Satan would be sifting the apostles like wheat. But what did Peter say? 'Thank you'? or 'Yes, I need your prayers'? No. He said 'Lord, I am ready to go with You, both to prison and to death' (v.33). After all that had happened, Peter refused to believe what Jesus was saying. 'I don't need prayer,' he thinks, 'whatever Jesus may say.'

But the worst thing about that meal was Judas. Judas is the archetypal bad guy for us, but at that time he was still Jesus' friend. He left that meal table, on his way to betray Jesus, and Jesus knew. Now, how do you think Jesus felt about that? Later, in the garden, Judas returned with the soldiers. He pointed Jesus out in the uncertain light by greeting him with a kiss. This kiss was a mark of their friendship. And Jesus greeted him:

'Friend' (Mt 26:50). The warmth of the kiss was still on Jesus' cheek as the soldiers closed in.

The prophetic Scriptures show us what Jesus felt: 'Even my own familiar friend in whom I trusted, who ate my bread, has lifted up his heal against me' (Ps 41:9); 'I am weary with my crying . . . I have become a stranger to my brothers . . . Reproach has broken my heart, and I am full of heaviness; I looked for someone to take pity, but there was none; and for comforters, but I found none . . . I am poor and sorrowful . . . ' (Ps 69:3, 8, 20, 29); 'In return for my love they are my accusers . . . I am poor and needy, and my heart is wounded within me' (Ps 109:4, 22). Do we think we can teach Jesus what betrayal feels like?

Before Judas arrived, Jesus waited and prayed in the garden. Naturally he wanted his closest friends around him. He told them how he felt: 'My soul is exceedingly sorrowful, even to death' (Mt 26:38), and he asked them to 'watch and pray, lest you enter into temptation' (v.41). You see, it was still others' needs that he thought of. But it would have been good, in his terrible grief, to have had his friends sharing his time of prayer. As it was, they fell asleep. Three times he woke them, but it was no good.

And then the soldiers were upon them. Here was a chance at last to prove their friendship for Jesus, but what happened? Peter became violent, and Jesus had to put the situation right by healing the wounded servant. Then they all ran away! So much for friendship.

Peter followed Jesus secretly, but his accent gave him away, and now he was in danger. He denied even knowing Jesus. At that moment, 'the Lord turned and looked at Peter' (Lk 22:61). We know how Peter felt because the Bible tells us he 'went out and wept bitterly' (v.62), but how did Jesus feel? Alone and friendless in the High Priest's house, he heard a familiar voice, and it was Peter disowning him!

Do we *really* need to teach Jesus about betrayal?

The support Jesus' friends gave him can be summed up in one sentence: 'They all forsook Him and fled' (Mk 14:50). And yet these apostles had accepted a calling 'that they might be with Him' (Mk 3:14). 'With Him' – not just in the good times, but all the time. Although Jesus is God the Son, he is also fully a man. And this man, in his time of terrifying need, was betrayed by all his friends. Of course, if you and I had been there we would have been entirely different. . . .

What about you and me?

What I am about to say now will seem very strange to some people. Perhaps I can explain it best by pointing to the prophet Hosea. You and I would get on well with Hosea. He too had an unfaithful partner. His wife, Gomer, was an adulteress. The whole experience taught him so much.

What did Hosea learn from his unfaithful wife? He learned what God feels about *his* unfaithful wife. Hosea's prophecy is largely a condemnation of unfaithful Israel: 'Bring charges against your mother, bring charges; for she is not My wife, nor am I her Husband! Let her put away her harlotries from her sight, and her adulteries from between her breasts' (Hos 2:2).

These are God's words, speaking as a betrayed husband. Read on and you will find anger, hurt, pleading, warning and, yes, betrayal. What has happened? God has taught a prophet what he, the Almighty God, feels about an unfaithful people. You and I can identify with Hosea, but what do you make of the phrase 'an

33

unfaithful people'? Can you identify with that too? I wish I couldn't.

Let me tell you one way I worked through my feelings of betrayal. I admitted an unpleasant truth: not only had I been betrayed, but I was also a betrayer. Yes, I have been faithful to Jesus, the church's Husband, but not all the time. He has been a perfect Husband to me, but I have not been a perfect wife to him. However, the church owes it to him to be a perfect wife. All sin is unfaithfulness.

'Adulterers and adulteresses! Do you not know that friendship with the world is enmity with God?' (Jas 4:4). Loving God means pleasing him, obeying him in everything. The attractions of the world – the desires of our flesh – these must yield to Christ's higher claim. The devil is constantly working to tempt us away from faithful love of God. Where he succeeds, we have betrayed our Lord.

It wouldn't have helped to slide into a pit of self-loathing. Perhaps I nearly did, but as it was, I rose up to breathe the clear air of honesty. I hadn't been as true to Jesus as I ought, but instead of crushing me, this confession allowed me to draw close to him, without pretence. And it gave me a new focus: how wonderful Jesus is to befriend a betrayer such as I!

This is not something I could face if it wasn't for God's amazing love and forgiveness. Isn't it wonderful to know we are forgiven! It means we can face up to the truth about ourselves. Let us see what it tells us about this in the Scriptures.

In Luke 7 we read of how Jesus was invited to a Pharisee's house for a meal. The Pharisees were – outwardly at least – the most respectable, religious and righteous people of the day. These meals were semi-public, so folk could wander in and watch. On this occasion someone came in and did more than watch. As was the custom, Jesus was lying on a couch, leaning on his elbow, eating, with his feet behind him, away from the table. A woman came in 'and stood at His feet behind Him weeping; and she began to wash His feet with her tears, and wiped them with the hair of her head; and she kissed His feet and anointed them with the fragrant oil' (v.38). It was normal to wash people's feet, because the dusty roads made sandalled feet dirty, however clean they had been on leaving home. Actually, the Pharisee should have done it for Jesus. But imagine a woman getting all that dirt on her clean hair! Imagine the tears flowing so freely that no water was needed. Imagine kissing Jesus' feet, because your love is flowing more freely even than the tears. And the fragrant oil would not have been cheap.

It must be wonderful to love Jesus like that! How did she come to love him so much? The fact is, as the Pharisee well knew, this was a very sinful woman. In response to the Pharisee's accusations Jesus put a question to him: if two men were let off their debts, which would love the lender more? 'I suppose,' the Pharisee replied, 'the one whom he forgave more.' Jesus pointed out how loving the woman had been. This proved that she must have been forgiven a great deal, since she loved a great deal. 'Therefore I say to you, her sins, which are many, are forgiven, for she loved much. But to whom little is forgiven, the same loves little' (v.47).

Christ's death is of such inestimable value. It covers all our sins, even the worst, with great ease. But how many sins do we bring to Christ? How sinful do we believe ourselves to be? The Pharisee apparently thought he had only a few sins to be forgiven. The woman had 'sins which are many' – and knew it. But all were freely forgiven – *all of them*. No wonder she loved Jesus so much. However, it is not more sins we need, but rather to be aware of the sins we do have. And as we realise how much God forgives, our love for him grows.

Jesus has met with and comforted me. I was reeling with being betrayed, but I poured it all out to Jesus, the one whom I had betrayed by my every sin and short-coming. I was astonished to see my sins in a new light. Now I knew how God feels about betrayal. Why do I love him more now? Because I have seen more of my sin fully forgiven.

Have I really betrayed God?

May I invite you along the same road – that honesty road? I shall, because I am so glad of that road myself.

When we committed ourselves to Christ, we took on some obligations. We repented of our sins, and under-took to believe his word. The understanding was that we shouldn't keep sinning, and we would keep believ-ing. We knew that our salvation had been very expen-sive for Jesus, and that he had gone through astonishing agonies to pay for our guilt. At times we have been vividly aware of the immense price he paid. Let us watch Jesus again, as he carries our immense burden.

We see Jesus staggering painfully towards Calvary. His back is lacerated by the whipping, and he is wearing a crown, but it's made only of thorns, and that's why his head is bleeding. The bruises on his face are not serious, but they resulted from a session he had with the soldiers. The soldiers had a great time ridiculing Jesus. They blindfolded him and played a game whereby he had to guess which soldier had hit him.

Jesus has trouble walking, which is not really very surprising. So a bystander has to give him a hand carrying the cross. Then see him hanging there: naked, nailed to the cross; an object of hatred, contempt and ridicule. You'd have thought that the excruciating torture of crucifixion was enough, without everybody ridiculing him as well. And where were his disciples? Gone.

It's easy to condemn the disciples. Surely we would have stayed with Jesus. But let's try to understand them. They had their own priorities, which included staying alive, keeping out of prison and protecting their families. That's why they could only go so far with Jesus.

But am I so very different? Have I stuck with Jesus through everything, or have I only gone so far with him?

We all have different priorities and we love so many things, and in the midst of all that, there is sin. This doesn't trouble us as much as it ought.

Then there is the anxiety. Our faith has faltered more than once. How often have our faith and obedience made Christ first in our lives? Well, not often enough. Have we betrayed him? Have we failed to live up to our commitment?

How contradictory we are! One moment we can feel so much in love with Jesus that we would do anything or go anywhere with him; then, minutes later, he is forgotten, crowded out by other matters. One moment, like Peter, we would make any sacrifice for him; the next, this little sin or that little compromise denies him afresh. We really love him – we really do – but, like the apostles, we can't stay awake to spend an hour with him, 'watching and praying'.

Yes, he forgives us, but he wants us to know what is forgiven. Betrayal. And now we know how bad that is.

What about our betrayal?

Perhaps the one who is gone isn't so different from you after all. Yes, your love did betray you, but you have done your share of betraying. You have betrayed the most wonderful person of all. And he gave you – gives you – no reason to betray him. That's something you can't say to Lee.

But things are different now. Now you know what betrayal feels like. What use should you make of this new knowledge? Should you use it to blame the one who has gone? That would make you feel better about yourself. Or should you leave Lee to God's judgement – better yet, to God's mercy? Who will throw the first stone at Lee? Surely someone innocent of betrayal themselves.

Yes, by all means keep thinking about betrayal, but think about *your* betrayal of Jesus. And think about his loving forgiveness. Ask for tears – the kind of tears that the sinful woman had when she washed Jesus' feet – and pray for grace to please him.

Isn't it remarkable how much God loves us, when we are so unworthy of that love? How willing, how eager, he is to do us good, when we have repaid his love so meanly! How good it is to stand before him, traitors in ourselves, but everlastingly loved in Christ! If we look at it like this, 'betrayed' may become a word that makes us glad. It will make us cry, like the sinful woman, but it will fill us with love and joy too.

3

Why?

'Why?' That is the question everybody asks. You've heard it a thousand times: 'Why did it have to rain?' 'Why did the car have to break down so far from home?' 'Why pick on me?' Usually there's a note of 'It isn't fair' that comes with the 'why?' 'Why did this have to happen to *me*?' 'What have I done to deserve this?'

Well, now it's your turn. 'Why?' seems a very good question now, doesn't it? Why you? What have you done to deserve it? Of course you're only human. No doubt there are many things you've done wrong, but compared with everyone else you're not such a bad person. In fact you're rather better than most. You're not bragging, you're simply stating a fact.

There are a lot of things you are not. You are not unfaithful; you are not a thief, a liar, violent or abusive; you are not irresponsible, lazy or totally selfish – at least, not normally. Everyone has their weak moments. The point is, you do know people who *are* like this, most of the time, and their partners haven't gone off. So why is that?

Is this how you've been thinking? Or is it more like this: 'I know why it happened. This is the punishment I've been expecting. I can't blame God. It's what I've earned'? Why? What have you done? 'It's everything. I'm such a useless person. I'm a rotten Christian.' So you haven't done anything terrible? 'My whole life has been terrible.'

Which way have you been thinking? Both? Well, that's not as strange as it might sound. Both trains of thought may have been going round and round in your head, and you may have wondered if you were going mad with it all. You may still wonder whether it should be, 'Why did this happen to me?' or, 'It's all my fault.'

The trouble with 'It's all my fault' is that it leads to 'If only'. 'If only' is a real killer. 'If only I had done that differently.' 'If only I had given in on that issue.' 'If only I had prayed more.' You analyse everything, and find a way you could have done better. Could you, by some quite minor change of course, have avoided this whole disaster? Perhaps. You don't know, but you go on torturing yourself, going over it again and again.

And it's such an awful, lonely feeling. You seem to stand alone in an unfriendly universe, unable to avoid horrible things happening to you. You ask the universe 'Why?', but it doesn't answer. You can't bring it to justice. You can't, by living a decent life, guarantee that awful things won't happen again. If it did this to you, what else is in store? And what can you do to avoid it? Not much, it would seem. You're on your own, apparently, with no control over your destiny.

If it *was* all your own fault, that is no better. The universe has punished you, and how strict and harsh it is! For your faults – and surely they weren't major crimes – a crippling price has been exacted. There has been no sympathy, no kindness, no mercy. Now you know that disasters will happen again, unless you can become, well, virtually perfect. And how can you do that?

That is such a lonely feeling too. You are not alone; you share the universe with a judge who is pitilessly just. It would be better to be alone.

It is high time we looked at the Bible.

Isn't it strange how the memory works? When you're ill, you remember previous illnesses more vividly. Toothache brings the last visit to the dentist to mind. I remember a vivid mental picture I had, many years ago, when I was terribly unhappy. I was alone then, and crying out to God in my unhappiness. It seemed that he wasn't doing anything to help. He was just standing there while I was suffering.

Then I saw the picture. It was of me, only I was a small child. I was crying and complaining, and a man was holding me. He was both bearded and grey with the wisdom of age and strong and capable with the energy of youth. I knew it was my heavenly Father. He was holding me, cradling me in his arms. He was doing nothing else, because nothing else could be done. Except there was something else: he was crying too. He was sharing my misery. It seemed to me then that it would be better to stop complaining. It would be better to return the love of this wise and mighty God – this God who loved me, however ugly my mood might be.

My pain didn't grow less, but I ceased to feel alone in a pointless universe. I knew that God's mighty power, matchless wisdom and unconditional love were at work, and that somehow I was on the receiving end of great benefits. I just didn't know what they were. But then I didn't need to know.

From that time on, my mind was open to see what the Bible says about God's control of his creation. Not that the Bible isn't clear enough, but our twentieth-century education has taught most of us something very different. We have been taught to see the control of everyday events in other hands.

God in control

We live in a world that is trying to push the knowledge of God aside. It is hardly surprising that he is not acknowledged as Creator and Controller of it. Other gods must be found to take his place. These gods – faceless, impersonal and harsh – are preferred to the true and living God.

Ancient pagans believed in the chance evolution of the world. They needed no god to explain it; chance was their god. Not only had chance brought everything into being, it also controlled it. Their good news was that no God existed to punish sin, thus they could feel free to do as they wished. The bad news was that merciless chance controlled their destinies. This old belief has returned for many nowadays. They call her 'Lady Luck', but she's no lady. They believe that luck is merely random chance events. 'Your partner left you? That's bad luck.' Something even worse may happen next week. Who says lightning doesn't strike twice in the same place? Luck does not always observe the law of averages.

Other pagans believed in a balance of power. Good and evil struggled eternally, with one then the other controlling events on earth. In Christian circles this notion has returned as: God did this, the devil did that. The devil is seen to be out of God's control sometimes. Bad events are of the devil; good events are from God. 'Your partner left you? That was the devil.' God couldn't really stop the devil. God had to relinquish control – maybe because of your sins, maybe because of the 'prayers' of the local witches' coven, maybe because you (or others) don't pray enough. How can I comfort you? If the devil had a free hand once, how can I tell you he won't again? What will he do next time? What a shame our God is so powerless!

A more recent view is that God did create all things – but. . . . But he made the universe like a machine. Having made it, he stepped aside and left it to run automatically, thus we are really in the power of an impersonal machine. Its mechanics, laws and inevitability are in control. God is 'out to lunch'. But you can't ask a machine for mercy. You can't tell it you've had enough, and beg it for kindness. The machine, like the law of gravity, operates relentlessly. Your wife left you? Presumably you, maybe others too, have done things that inevitably led to that sad event. It is no good saying that you have behaved reasonably well, because an evil result proves an evil cause. If you are suffering, you must have sinned.

Many Christians, without realising it, have adopted one or other of these beliefs – or even a bit of all of them. Mixed in with the Bible, it produces a sad muddle. But this is no time – if ever there was a time – to be muddled. The questions are urgent: 'Why?' 'Is it my fault?' 'Will disasters keep happening to me?' 'Am I alone with a merciless or meaningless universe?' And the answers need to be good.

'And we know that all things work together for good to those who love God, to those who are called according to His purpose' (Rom 8:28). Ah, at last! Something solid to grasp; something true, loving, merciful, kind and immeasurably powerful. God, who loves us, is in absolute control. Not chance, but God. 'Our God is in heaven; He does whatever He pleases' (Ps 115:3). 'Whatever the Lord pleases He does, in heaven and in earth' (Ps 135:6). God 'works all things according to the counsel of His will' (Eph 1:11). Christ is 'upholding all things by the word of His power' (Heb 1:3). If he stopped doing so, everything would fall apart or cease to exist. It is no harder for him to hold open the Red Sea than it is to keep it in its normal existence.

The Book of Job is all about suffering. Job was 'blameless and upright, and one who feared God and shunned evil' (Job 1:1). The devil was certainly instrumental in Job's sufferings, but he could do nothing without God's express permission. *Nothing!* Jesus said: 'All authority has been given to Me in heaven and on earth' (Mt 28:18). Note that it is *'all* authority', and that it is specifically 'on earth'. This tells me that there is no balance of power. Jesus is Lord! The devil gained permission to wreak disasters on Job (chps 2–3). The devil's motives were malicious, but God remained in control throughout. God had other purposes, loving purposes, and they controlled the events.

Do you feel that the devil has gained control over your circumstances? Well, he hasn't. God never surrenders control.

Job suffered terribly, and he expressed his pain vividly. That is good. Expressing grief is part of the prayers of the Bible: 'Behold, these are the ungodly, who are always at ease; they increase in riches. Surely I have cleansed my heart in vain . . . ' says Asaph. Because, unlike these bad people, 'All day long I have been plagued, and chastened every morning' (Ps 73:12–14). Does this sound a bit like you? Why did this happen to you, and not to people so much worse than you?

'You are the God of my strength; why do You cast me off? Why do I go mourning because of the oppression of

44

the enemy?' (Ps 43:2). If you feel that God has deserted you, tell him. Better to speak to him from the heart, however wrong you are, than to pretend.

'I am troubled, I am bowed down greatly; I go mourning all the day long. . . . Do not forsake me, O Lord; O my God, be not far from me!' (Ps 38:6, 21). When they felt awful, they told God. Don't feel guilty about it.

Job's friends were initially very sympathetic to Job's distress. Then they changed. They thought that Job's suffering must mean Job had sinned, just as if a machine controlled the universe: so much suffering meant so much sin. 'Had you been righteous, Job,' they said, 'this wouldn't have happened to you.'

Of course, Job knew that God punishes the wicked. Job said: 'This is the portion of a wicked man with God . . . Terrors overtake him like a flood' (Job 27:13, 20). Job's friends behaved 'with complete nonsense' (v.12), because they thought this happened automatically and immediately. Actually, God runs things personally, delaying judgement and restoration for our good. Yes, the wicked are punished in the long run. Yes, the righteous are vindicated eventually. Job was vindicated, but not until later.

It's bad enough not knowing why. Has someone hinted that they know why? It's your fault? Oh, that makes it so much worse. It's easy for them, with their mechanical universe, to make their simplistic judgement, but it's hard for you to carry it along with everything else.

A doctor friend of mine is in charge of a hospice for terminal care. He told me that evangelical Christians – folk like himself – can find it harder to die than others. I was surprised, and asked why. 'They feel that they're letting the side down by not being healed,' he told me. I have often thought about that since. Have we added to the miseries of the miserable?

I think there can be a false picture of the Christian. He is free from sorrows and grief, disasters and miseries. These things threaten him, but he prays for deliverance, and they pass him by. A pain-free Christian! Where this picture has been painted, devastated Christians are an embarrassment, so the pain-free Christian treats them (unconsciously) with embarrassment. Not only are they in pain, there is something wrong with them.

Thank God for the Bible! When we feel the embarrassment of the pain-free Christian, we can look at the Bible Christian. Enoch died young. Job lost everything. Abraham and Sarah were childless. Moses was an outcast. Samuel's children were criminal. David's first marriage broke up. Hosea was suddenly single. Jesus was executed a criminal. They all 'let the side down'. There was hardly a saint in Scripture who wasn't afflicted with misery at some point. This doesn't make you and me great, but it puts us in great company. Far from letting the side down, it is a mark of being on the right side. 'We must through many tribulations enter the kingdom of God' (Acts 14:22).

Not that our unhappiness hasn't taught us something about our own sinfulness, but 'to him who is afflicted, kindness should be shown by his friend' (Job 6:14).

All this increased Job's distress. He knew that God – not chance – was in control, and this meant that his sufferings were under God's control. But he also knew, he thought, that he was a righteous man, whatever his imperfections. Did this suffering mean that he was a hypocrite after all? Surely not! But how else could he explain things?

Job could find no explanation, but with the passage of

time, God's purpose became clear. The 'Why?' received an answer – or part of an answer, at least.

The answer to the 'Why?'

God appeared to Job and he showed Job how little he knew. In chapters 38–41 he questioned Job about the intricacies of the universe. Why did he do this? Because we need to know how little we know.

'Oh, the depth of the riches both of the wisdom and knowledge of God! How unsearchable are His judgments and His ways past finding out!' (Rom 11:33). 'Unsearchable', 'past finding out'! The universe is such an amazing place. There is so much that is unknown, but even the most ignorant of us can enjoy its beauty and richness. God is in control of it. We can appreciate that fact. We can see his hand at work and know what he is doing – sometimes. Much of the time, however, we don't know why. In that sense we are like children. We know that Dad has it all under control, but we don't really understand how he runs things.

God is the loving Father; we the tiny children. He can't make us understand the 'whys' but he wants us to understand that 'all things work together for good to those who love God, to those who are called according to His purpose' (Rom 8:28). He wants us to know that he loves us, and that everything is under control.

Asaph, whom I quoted earlier, became very unhappy when he couldn't understand why, 'until I went into the sanctuary of God' (Ps 73:17). There, drawing close to God, he understood. He still didn't understand everything, but he understood this: 'I am continually with You; You hold me by my right hand' (v.23). This is a truly wonderful insight. When we ask 'Why?', we usually feel so alone, so unloved. Then we see that while we were crying hopelessly, he was holding us; while we were feeling alone and confused, really he was loving and protecting us; while we were complaining, he was loving. 'I was so foolish and ignorant' (v.22) – 'You hold me by my right hand' (v.23).

No wonder that his love for God burst forth anew! 'Whom have I in heaven but You? And there is none upon earth that I desire besides You' (v.25). God still loves us, in spite of all our moans and complaints. He is holding us and caring for us at our most wretched. God *is* in control; he is *not* aloof from our pain.

Job received a marvellous blessing. 'Behold, I am vile,' he declared (Job 40:4). 'Vile' (in the original) means 'of no account, a nobody'. Job was seeing what all of us would love to see: a glorious appearance of the God who loves us so much. God actually spoke to him! It was easy to acknowledge that in comparison with God he was a nobody. All doubts were stilled: 'I know that You can do everything, and that no purpose of Yours can be withheld from You,' he told his Lord (42:2). His Father was in absolute control.

'I have heard of You by the hearing of the ear,' said Job, 'but now my eye sees You' (42:5). His previous knowledge of God, whereby he was such a godly man, seemed mere hearsay. Now he saw God. In that marvellous moment it would have been impossible for Job to regret the suffering, but Job's loving Father hadn't finished.

Everything was restored to Job. His reputation: God told Job's friends that Job was right and they were wrong (42:7–9). His prosperity: he received twice what he lost (vv.10, 12). His social circle: Job was suddenly the centre of his social circle again (v.11). His family: he had children again (v.13).

Yes, in time it all made more sense. Some of those 'whys' received answers. Job was glad that God was in control, and sorry that he had criticised God's policy.

So . . . ?

God loves us so much, and is holding us tightly. It's all right to cry, as a child. It's all right to ask 'Why?' Know that his love controls all things. This disaster wasn't 'bad luck'. It wasn't the devil out of control. It wasn't your sin. It happened, and you don't need to know why. You probably wouldn't understand the answer anyway.

In my greatest unhappiness, this truth was a solitary rock in a maelstrom of misery and confusion. I was like a shipwrecked man in a storm. Violent waves struck me on every side, and I was covered with bruises. Nothing was visible in the darkness, and the only thing that kept me from drowning was this one rock: God loved me in spite of everything, and he was in complete control. Here was something I could hold on to, or rather something that held on to me. Without it I would have drowned.

It makes all the difference if God is in control. You can look back at your marriage and know that God was in control. The good years you had together *were* good years. You don't have to let the present poison the past. God gave you those good years. They are a scrapbook with many good memories in it. The book is closed, but it doesn't have to be destroyed or thrown away. What a waste that would be – to make so many years of your life meaningless! They weren't meaningless. God gave them to you. You don't want to look at the scrapbook? Of course you don't! Put it away in the attic. You'll want it one day, and it'll be there.

Since God is in control, who knows what will happen? God is able to bring Lee back. Does that seem impossible? 'With God nothing will be impossible' (Lk 1:37). But here you must be wise. There are hidden dangers lurking. On the one hand, we doubt the great things God can do; we close the door or burn the bridge, when God might have brought Lee back. But there is an opposite danger. We might keep pining, and there is great danger in pining. After an amputation, it is important to let the wound heal. A surgeon would hardly keep the wound open in a vain hope of the lost limb being reattached. This would threaten the very life of the patient.

Perhaps we have spoken to our non-Christian friends, and they have told us, 'They never come back. Don't waste your time hoping. Get on with your life! Make a fresh start!' But they don't know that God is in control. Meanwhile, our Christian friends are full of faith. They tell us, 'Don't give up hope. We're all praying she'll come back.' How can you start healing while they are still praying?

Thank God most of our Christian friends don't know what it is like. They haven't experienced being suddenly single – and we wouldn't wish the experience on anyone – but because of this they can't see the danger of hanging on 'in faith' when it is time to heal.

We want to do the right thing. We don't want to disobey God, so we listen to our believing friends. The trouble is, they can't imagine what it is like. They can't imagine how the amputation can be complete in 'so short a time'. So short a time? It hasn't felt that way to us. It seems like years have passed in the space of weeks. 'God hates divorce,' they remind us. We must keep the wound open for more weeks of years.

'The Lord God of Israel says that He hates divorce' (Mal 2:16). Why? 'The Lord has been witness between you and the wife of your youth, with whom you have dealt treacherously; yet she is your companion and your wife by covenant' (v.14). What does God hate? It is the treachery of dismissing the faithful wife. This doesn't mean the faithful believer must welcome the adulterer back.

What does the Bible say? Certainly sexual immorality is legitimate ground for divorce (Mt 19:9). It is not that you refuse to forgive, but the marriage covenant – the oneness – has been broken. You are not obliged to have Lee back, although you may. It turns on repentance. If the adulterer returns, will the same thing happen again? Are you simply perpetuating the misery? Have they repented, or have they simply regretted the sin?

'Godly sorrow produces repentance leading to salvation' (2 Cor 7:10). This 'godly sorrow' has vivid symptoms: 'diligence . . . clearing of yourselves . . . indignation . . . fear . . . vehement desire . . . zeal . . . vindication' (v.11). You can't mistake it. It is strong, passionate, full-blooded and eager to prove its sincerity. By contrast, 'the sorrow of the world produces death' (v.10). It is merely a worldly regret – it doesn't feel its guilt before God. It couldn't pray the fifty-first Psalm. It just regrets having done it. It hopes, promises, it won't do it again . . . but it might.

The faithful partner needs to know whether it is repentance or regret. We need help to assess these things. The right kind of help may lead a regretful adulterer on to repentance, and this process shouldn't be hurried.

Is there a point beyond which you can't have Lee back? Yes. Deuteronomy 24 visualises a situation in which a woman has been given a 'certificate of divorce', and has left her husband. She then 'goes and becomes another man's wife' (v.2 – 'wife' is not in the original). If this new relationship ends – perhaps with the man dying – is it possible to remarry the original husband? 'Her former husband who divorced her must not take her back to be his wife' (v.4). So, remarriage makes the original marriage impossible to restart – ever.

Does this mean a legal remarriage or a common-law 'remarriage'? After all, people often live together as man and wife without being legally married. Perhaps even while there are legal delays to the divorce the unfaithful partner lives in a common-law marriage with another. In Deuteronomy 24, only the first man is called the 'husband' (v.4). The second man is just called 'man', even in verse 3 where the English translation has 'latter husband'. The Hebrew is 'latter man'. So she may or may not be legally married to the second man. All we are told is that she has been served with a certificate of divorce. Then, 'She has departed from his [her ex-husband's] house, and goes and becomes another man's.'

It has gone beyond an affair; Lee is married (whether legally or in common law) to another. Lee is in the same position as the woman in Deuteronomy 24, who is 'his woman'. *That* is the point of no return. 'If a man divorces his wife, and she goes from him and becomes another man's, may he return to her again? Would not that land be greatly polluted?' (Jer 3:1).

Clearly, then, God puts an end to pining. There comes a time when the wound must close, and be healed. Christians shouldn't pray for marital reconciliation beyond that point.

But perhaps you haven't got to that point. Now is the

time for telling Lee that all is forgiven and you want Lee home again. You're sorry too. There are lots of things you would have done – will do – differently. You need to talk. You need help. There are certain mutual friends, or marriage guidance agencies. The marriage has taken a terrible battering; all the glow has been bashed off it. You may not feel like making the vast effort needed to restore it, but, for the children's sake. . . .

Then again, maybe the differences seem irreconcilable. You can't see how the marriage can be healed, even if you both said all the 'sorrys' in the world; even if all the pride were surrendered. *But God is in control!*

And with God nothing is impossible!

4
Revenge

'It's natural enough to want revenge.' Is that what
you're thinking? You've been hurt, badly hurt, so why
shouldn't you get back at the one who hurt you? Stop! I
know you wouldn't actually *do* anything – well, not
much beyond a few well-chosen words, minor actions,
petty acts of vengeance.

But it's your thoughts I'm talking about. What are
you saying to Lee or doing to Lee in your thoughts?
What's that? They are only fantasies? What you think
stays in your mind and can't do any harm? Well, you
know that isn't true! You know enough bitter people,
don't you? Haven't you seen their innermost bitterness
as plainly as if it were written on their foreheads?

You'll be seeing your 'ex' from time to time, because
you'll need to talk about the children, money, the house
. . . . How will Lee find you? Bitter and vengeful? Cold
and unforgiving?

I wonder who prays for Lee now. Do you? Or is it,
'Lord, strike Lee down!'?

You say you have reason. Well, perhaps we ought to
talk about that. No, wait! I'm not going to blame it all
on you. Not after what I've said about Job. But I'd like
to say a little about Jesus. He suffered too, you know.

Ah, but you know what I'm going to say. Jesus suffered and forgave, and we must too. And you're not too impressed by that. You'd like to remind me about something too. Doesn't the Bible talk about punishment for sinners? Don't the psalmists ask God to sort out the wicked?

Well, yes, I know that. But perhaps you should let me say what I was going to say. Perhaps you haven't really thought enough about Jesus.

Why Jesus suffered

There was nothing wrong with man as he came fresh from the Creator's hands. 'Truly, this only I have found: that God made man upright, but they have sought out many schemes' (Eccl 7:29). When Adam and Eve first sinned, *God went looking for them*: 'And they heard the sound of the Lord God walking in the garden in the cool of the day, and Adam and his wife hid themselves from the presence of the Lord God among the trees of the garden. Then the Lord God called to Adam and said to him, "Where are you?"' (Gen 3:8–9).

Why did he do that? Why did he not give them what they so richly deserved? Yes, they were punished, but God gave them that wonderful promise of Christ coming to defeat our enemy (Gen 3:15).

Why did God bear with the continual infidelity of his people? How often did he come and rescue them, and, no sooner were they safe, than they turned again to the demonic idols? And yet he would rescue them again! Why?

This is the continually recurring theme of the Old Testament. God even commissioned a prophet, Hosea, to marry an unfaithful woman in order that he should experience first hand the miseries of having an unfaithful wife. And he did this so that Hosea could understand something of what God felt. 'Go,' the Lord said, 'take yourself a wife of harlotry and children of harlotry, for the land has committed great harlotry by departing from the Lord' (Hos 1:2).

Have you found that people can't really understand what you are going through because they haven't gone through it themselves? Has it occurred to you that that is how God felt? He found that we couldn't understand. He made a good, happy and fruitful world for man to enjoy, yet what did he get in return? Rebellion, disobedience, open contempt. Man chose the devil, evil and ugly as he is, rather than God.

His own people – Israel, the church – were not so different. Even the best of us have rebelled so often. We have disobeyed, chosen Satan. But he has a special relationship with us. Christ is our husband, we are his wife. And our unfaithfulness hurts all the more for it.

God wanted Hosea to feel it. What was Hosea's wife like? I think that she was an ordinary woman in a society much like our own. It is terrifyingly common for girls, even Christian girls, to sleep around before marriage. Acceptable as this may seem today, God says of such: 'She has done a disgraceful thing in Israel, to play the harlot in her father's house' (Deut 22:21). This certainly appears strange to us because we see 'mild' sexual immorality as a million miles from prostitution. Not so with God.

I think that Hosea's wife was 'a harlot' in this sense rather than a full-blown prostitute. After all, Leviticus 21:7 says: 'They shall not take a wife who is a harlot . . . for the priest is holy to his God.' This applies to priests, and Hosea is not said to be a priest. However, it seems to me likely that it has a general reference to all public representatives of God – prophet as well as priest. If so, then the woman Hosea married was an ordinary representative of an immoral society.

Perhaps he feared for what she would do, but I imagine that he loved her, and had high hopes for their life together. Perhaps they had a 'good' marriage. After all, we know that 'good' marriages can be betrayed as easily as 'bad' ones. No doubt he did his best in the marriage – better than many who aren't betrayed.

What did he feel when his wife began to be unfaithful? Perhaps we can guess. But it was so that the prophet (and through him we too) could understand how God felt all along. God has been a perfect husband. His patience, his generosity, his pure and shining love have never lapsed for a second. How do you think he feels?

However, God is the world's Judge too, and he commissioned the prophet to prosecute faithless Israel. 'Bring charges against your mother, bring charges; for she is not My wife, nor am I her Husband! Let her put away her harlotries from her sight, and her adulteries from between her breasts' (Hos 2:2).

Surely this was it: God's extraordinary patience had run out! But no. 'How can I give you up, Ephraim? How can I hand you over, Israel? . . .' My heart churns within Me; My sympathy is stirred. . . . I will heal their backsliding, I will love them freely' (Hos 11:8; 14:4). The Bible continues to be full of grace, mercy and forgiveness. And when we come to the New Testament, it is all the more extraordinary. Long-prophesied new degrees of undeserved love and unimaginable kindness are now poured out. And the plan has become much wider. The Jews, by this time, had been cured of idol-worship. They were now a people based on the Holy Book. As imperfect as they were, they were a race of saints compared with the idolatrous, demonic nations that made up the rest of the world. These nations, steeped in demonic darkness, were surely beyond hope. With their many crimes, over many generations, how could a holy God even want to do them any good?

But that was the plan. God would call many from these benighted nations into the fullest intimacy of his fatherly love. Not revolted by the dark hues of their sin, his love reached out unperturbed.

How they fought him! Vicious and bloody persecutions flung the love of God back in his face, but 300 years after his resurrection, Jesus received the submission of the Roman Empire. Watered continually by the blood of martyrs, challenged continually by the force of truth, the demonic empire had crumbled. Reluctantly, they bowed to Christ. And many received the salvation of their souls.

I'm still asking, 'Why such relentless love which will not take "no" for an answer?'

Perhaps you can continue the story in your own life. How long did you live in rebellion against God before you bowed the knee to him? And have you been unfaithful to him since then? Ah, I see you have. And he forgave you? Freely, fully? Perhaps you felt his eagerness to restore you to the closeness of his loving embrace? Didn't you wonder why he was more eager to forgive you than you were to confess? And how many times have you sinned against him since? Would you care to count? No?

'Who is a God like You, pardoning iniquity and passing over the transgression of the remnant of His heritage? He does not retain His anger forever, because He delights in mercy. He will again have compassion on us, and will subdue our iniquities. You will cast all our sins into the depths of the sea' (Mic 7:18–19).

The sea mentioned here reminds us of Solomon's 'Sea' (2 Chron 4:2–5). This was a massive water container for cleansing those who entered the Holy Place. It was absurdly large, containing about 8,000 gallons. Imagine seeing this Sea. As you are cleansed to enter the Holy Place, see where the cleansing comes from. It towers above you, this great Sea. Forgiveness, cleansing, atonement poured upon you; not by the cupful, nor the bathful, but like a great ocean. Such is our God, who 'delights in mercy', and 'will cast all our sins into the depths of the sea'.

How willing he is to forget our sins! 'For I will be merciful to their unrighteousness,' he declares, 'and their sins and their lawless deeds I will remember no more' (Heb 8:12). God, who knows everything, has chosen to be ignorant of one thing: our forgiven sin. He has simply forgotten it all.

This wonderful grace! This free forgiveness! This great love that sought and found us and wouldn't let us go! It is entirely free. Free to us, that is. It was anything but free for Christ, for it was he who had to pay for it.

The price is paid

We should never speak glibly of Christ's sufferings. It wasn't easy for him, because he is God the Son. That's what made it much harder. The helps he might have had, as God the Son, he refused. 'Do you think,' he asked, 'that I cannot now pray to My Father, and He will provide Me with more than twelve legions of angels?' (Mt 26:53). It could have been easy, but it was actually much harder.

Many other men suffered the physical torments of crucifixion too. Others were whipped, humiliated, deserted and tortured. But none had the sin of the world put on their shoulders, and none could feel a tithe – not a millionth – of his disgust at sin.

Jesus really hates sin. That's why he never ever committed it. He never felt its clammy defilement. Never, that is, until he became the worst person in the world. 'For He made Him who knew no sin to be sin for us, that we might become the righteousness of God in Him' (2 Cor 5:21). *He was made sin for us*! Just think what that must have meant.

Surely the other tortures, physical and emotional, were nothing beside this! That thing he most hated, utterly loathed, totally rejected – he became it.

The whole Trinity hates sin. It is impossible for the Trinity to be divided, but it is also impossible that the Trinity should sin. So when the Son became sin, he had to be separated from the Father. 'Jesus cried out with a loud voice, saying, "Eli, Eli, lama sabachthani?" that is, "My God, My God, why have You forsaken Me?"' (Mt 27:46).

What did this mean? We cannot know. Nor would we understand. But this much is clear: it was terrible beyond words for Jesus. For Jesus – not for us – because it happened to him so that it wouldn't happen to us. Of course it didn't just 'happen' to Jesus. He had willed and planned it. He wanted to do it, so eager is he to forgive us. He had tasted its agonies in the Garden of Gethsemane, because he knew what was going to happen.

What did the Father feel? What would we have felt if it had been our son? It doesn't bear thinking about. It seems that God suffered more than it is possible for God to suffer.

And it wasn't even for good people. 'God demonstrates His own love toward us, in that while we were still sinners, Christ died for us . . . when we were enemies' (Rom 5:8, 10). Whatever our more optimistic appraisal of mankind, our Maker knew us to be sinners, his 'enemies'. This was no noble rescue of the 'good guys'; it was the 'bad guys' he rescued.

'Jesus said, "Father, forgive them, for they do not know what they do"' (Lk 23:34). I'm glad I'm forgiven, although 'glad' sounds a rather trivial word. My sin and rebellion have earned me hell a thousand times over, but God has befriended me – for eternity. No, 'glad' isn't really the word for it. I'm not glad that Jesus had to suffer so horribly, but if he hadn't, you and I would be lost for ever. So I *am* glad.

What about revenge?

Let's get the issue of justice and punishment out of the way. 'Beloved, do not avenge yourselves, but rather give place to wrath' (Rom 12:19). This means letting God's wrath deal with it. He goes on: 'For it is written, "Vengeance is Mine, I will repay," says the Lord.' Vengeance, and rewards for that matter, are God's business. He is in control of the universe, and he is quite capable of seeing to it. He tells us to get out of his way; that vengeance is his. We are told to 'give place' – to make room – for his wrath to operate. We must leave it up to him.

So what is our part? It is to forgive, as Jesus forgave us. Well, not exactly as Jesus forgave us. Jesus was tempted as we have been. He was entirely innocent and treated appallingly, yet he forgave – the innocent forgiving the guilty. But it's different for you and me, isn't it?

We are not innocent, and we certainly cannot say: 'Which of you convicts Me of sin?' (Jn 8:46) as Jesus could. Earlier Jesus had said: 'He who is without sin among you, let him throw a stone at her first' (Jn 8:7). *He who is without sin*! Is that you and me? Hardly! Therefore, when we forgive, it must be a little different.

We forgive because we are forgiven. We are not so different, after all, from those we forgive. But for God's grace, we would be as bad, worse. Like Jesus, we know about temptation, but unlike Jesus, we know about giving in to it.

We can understand the fierceness of temptations. How often we 'couldn't help' giving in to them. Forces too strong for us, it seemed, drove us to sin. We knew that we could overcome through Christ, but we also know that we didn't.

How must your 'ex' have felt? Lee had always held the marriage vows sacred. What strong temptations, inner compulsions, irresistible forces there must have been! What confusion! Did Lee pray for help? Did Lee feel a force too strong to overcome?

Is that how it felt for Lee? Perhaps. Well, you and I can understand all too well. We cannot excuse sin – God wants it forgiven, not excused – but it helps to sympathise with the weakness of a fellow sinner.

I am glad that I forgave. In releasing the one who hurt me, I found that I had released myself. I could stand before God, free. How could I have done that if I was refusing to give others the forgiveness that I needed for myself? How rich that release felt! I was no longer trapped by those revolving thoughts. There were no more accusations, revenge and bitter thoughts going round and round in my mind. Even as I came free, I could imagine what I might have suffered. My bitterness might have twisted and tortured me for ever. What a release!

I know you feel so full of hurt and anger against the one who left you. But keep forgiving Lee. Do you pray the Lord's Prayer daily? The Lord designed it for us, so it's the ideal outline. Use the 'As we forgive those who trespass against us'. Sometimes we have to do a lot of forgiving before we realise that we have forgiven.

In place of vengeance, let pity come. Don't think: 'Lee's got it all, and I'm left high and dry.' Think: 'What a dreadful sin to fall into! Lord, please draw Lee back to yourself.' And it *is* dreadful sin. Terrible consequences follow, and Lee needs God's grace desperately. Some in Lee's position never find it. At worst you have misery and loss, but nothing as terrible as this. Yes, you can pity Lee.

Is Lee's unfaithfulness clear to all? If it is, then I don't suppose Lee is getting the sympathy that you are. That can't be very easy for Lee: condemned from outside, guilty inside. Would you wish to swap places with Lee? Be like Jesus, who, in the midst of his own agony, could respond to that of another (Jn 19:26–27).

Pray for Lee's spiritual health. How does God bring about healing? Often through suffering. Perhaps Lee will experience some of the vengeance and wrath of God. You hope so – not because you wish Lee hurt, but because you wish Lee well; *spiritually* well. Pray that the Lord will restore Lee to himself. If Lee must suffer in the process, then at least let the process bring Lee back to God.

What sort of relationship?

If you have children, then you as parents will be seeing something of each other. The children need you both.

You mustn't speak ill of one another. That is too much of a burden for the children to carry. You must appear friendly. Where possible, you must praise Lee. After all, Lee has many good qualities. If you enlist the children's support against Lee, you will do them great damage. They are not called to be their parents' judges.

How tempting it is to slip in just one little remark; one little point! When the children ask you why you split up, what a release it would be to tell them. But consider first what you are building for the children.

You cannot now build them a united family, with their dad and mum. That is desperately sad, but it doesn't mean that all is lost. You can still build something. You can keep bitterness out of the building, which at least allows them to love their parents. Do that at least for your children.

Friends who have been suddenly single far longer than I tell me that they are glad of their sacrifice. They denied themselves the satisfaction of passing their bitterness on to the children, and from this sacrificial sowing, they have reaped a harvest. Their relationship with the past partner is now as good as it could be. This makes things as good as they could be for the children. Your sacrifice brings a future benefit for your children.

You and your 'ex' have separate lives, separate priorities, now. Gone is the time when you sought for the shared path together. You and Lee will disagree at times, each trying to persuade the other to fit in. If you had not forgiven Lee, your bitterness would seep out at such times. But you are forgiving Lee. What does this mean? Should you give way in a kindly manner?

No, forgiveness is not the same as being soft. We mustn't allow ourselves to be manipulated. Sometimes it is right to say 'no'. It isn't always kind to say 'yes'. But at least your 'no' is without venom and anger. It's 'no' because 'no' seems best – not because you want a petty revenge.

Perhaps your 'ex' will misinterpret you. Well, you can understand that. How could Lee expect forgiveness? How could Lee know that you are free?

5

Whose Fault?

I sometimes think we carry a law court around in our heads, and there is a long-running case in progress. Who is to blame for what has happened? You are being tried for every fault, every shortcoming, every weakness. Meanwhile, you are not inactive – you have some counter-suits in process. It was their fault, and you have evidence to support your case.

This court is always active, but sometimes it is extremely busy. Just recently, it has been humming with activity, very busy, working all hours. It has worked all night once or twice.

There has been an urgent case to hear: 'You vs Your "Ex"'. Who was to blame? You'd have thought, at a time like this, that there were more important things to worry about, such as how you will survive the blow, how you will go on living and whether you can build a new life. These are vital questions, so why fill your mind with an imaginary court case?

Unfortunately, we do not always do the logical, sensible thing, so perhaps you'd let me know how the case is going?

I understand that there has been lots of evidence presented. You are being accused of being a poor partner, and that it was your fault that Lee left. Well, what sort of evidence have they got? They are using some of the things Lee said after leaving? Well, perhaps you'll have something to answer to that. Anything else?

Ah, they've called your soul to the stand. It has testified of your relationship with God. It says that you haven't sought God, loved God, obeyed God as you ought. It says that it is your fault that you lack love and goodness; you didn't receive the supernatural help that marriage needs. You were selfish, not because you're only human, but because you refused heavenly assistance.

What will your defence attorney say to that? He's not sure? He says it's tough evidence to refute? It seems things are not looking very good for you.

The prosecution has called your memory to the stand, and it has testified damagingly against you. It remembers you taking Lee for granted and recalls how you were sometimes selfish, taken up with your own things, not sensitive to Lee's, and how you complained and were moody. It says you weren't much of a joy to live with. It has so much evidence to give. There are so many memories, and they're all ranged against you.

I'm glad to hear that your barrister has been determined, menacing even. He has cross-examined mercilessly, and no memory has left the witness stand without a thorough grilling. More than one has had to admit that there is much to say on your side. Some of the exchanges between prosecution and defence have been electric! And, of course, it wasn't *you* who left – that is a vital point!

Who do you think is winning? Perhaps it is hard to tell, with first one then the other seeming to gain the upper hand. Why is it taking so long to bring in the verdict?

How strange: the court is going over the same ground, over and over again, with the same questions bringing the same answers. Round and round, again and again. How can the case ever finish? And how can you endure the torture of endless accusation, endless self-justification?

The law court is more like a nightmare than a courtroom. At one moment you are the defendant, trying to establish your innocence. How can *you* be blamed, when *you* kept the marriage covenant? But suddenly you are a witness against yourself, testifying to a thousand little failings. Little they seemed, but together big enough to drive your love away. Then you are the jury, bringing in the 'guilty' verdict. And finally, worst of all, you are the judge, gleefully sentencing yourself to endless guilt and blame.

And all the time you are still the defendant, watching in horror as the net closes around you.

And then at other times you are prosecuting your own suit. It is Lee who is writhing in guilt as the evidence closes in. 'There was *one person*,' you thunder, 'who committed adultery!' What fierce joy you feel then! Suddenly the evidence points but one way, and you are fully exonerated. You stand tall, your actions justified.

Then the scene shifts, and once again you are in the dock, with the noose tightening around you. On and on it goes. Around and around, over and over. There must be a way of escape. Thank God, there is.

God and the law court

Yes, there is a law court, and not just in your imagination. What is more, it would find you guilty. But there's no need to worry because it would find Lee guilty too – although that isn't your business.

The remarkable thing is that it found Jesus guilty too. Yet we all know that he didn't do anything wrong. He stood in the dock and faced the evidence just as you do. And strangest of all, it was the same evidence! He stood accused of your crimes (mine too). Let's see what the Bible has to say about it all. Let's see why we needn't fear the law court.

Jesus died for our sins. This was possible because he became guilty of them: 'For He made Him who knew no sin to be sin for us, that we might become the righteousness of God in Him' (2 Cor 5:21). He 'knew no sin' – had never committed any sin – yet in spite of that, God made him to be sin. He *was* sin. What does this mean? He wasn't merely loaded with our sin, nor merely made sinful, but 'made sin'. I can't think of any stronger expression. Jesus actually became utterly guilty of sin, our sin. It was for us.

This meant that Jesus had to stand accused in the dock, really guilty. He was accused of all your sin, and mine. He had no defence. He pleaded guilty, and the sentence was crushing. The penalty was just. The eternal torments of hell – which you and I deserve – had to be suffered. Because Jesus is God, he could endure an eternity of torture in a limited space of time, so he finished the punishment we could never have finished.

We cannot imagine the horror of what he suffered. We cannot imagine the relief with which he said: 'It is finished!' (Jn 19:30). Finished! Or, you could translate it, 'Paid!' Because it was paid, all the guilt of our sins paid for in full.

Having paid for our sins, he need pay for them no more, and neither need we. Because he (though really innocent) stood guilty in the law court, we (really guilty) stand innocent. There is no sin of which we might be accused. Why? Because all our sins have been charged to Jesus. He pleaded guilty, was punished, and the case is closed.

I have known this for many years, but knowing it is not the same as knowing the power of it. A doctrine, once learned, can remain stored in the mind, and that's a good thing. But the power of it ebbs and flows. I remember, many years ago, singing 'When I survey the wondrous cross'. When we got to 'See from his head, his hands, his feet; sorrow and love flow mingled down . . .' I remember crying. The power of the doctrine broke me. At other times, I've taught the doctrine without the power. Some listening would be drinking of the life-giving waters, while my soul remained parched.

It so happened that before the blow fell on me, God empowered this doctrine to me. I had no idea that any blow might be hanging over me. I was watching *Ben Hur*, the classic film set in first-century Palestine. Ben Hur, the hero, is a thoroughly decent man. He is rich, a prince among the Jews. Then, out of the blue, a blow falls that all but destroys him. His family is thrown into the terrible dungeon, and he is driven across the desert to be a galley slave. Ben Hur is utterly miserable, and yet worse misery befalls him. They come to a Jewish village, and the slaves are given water, but Ben Hur has excited the malice of the Roman officer, who says: 'Not for him,' when the cup is passed to Ben Hur.

This is a moment of blackest misery. Ben Hur is the most wretched figure, and he sinks to the dust, covered with rags and wounds, broken and beaten. 'God, help me,' he murmurs, through parched lips, his face now in the dust.

Then we see the back of a man coming out of his shop. It is a carpenter's shop. He begins to splash water on the wretched man's face. Ben Hur looks up to see a face he does not recognise. Later in the film, he will see the same man again, dying for the sin of the world. For now, he drinks gratefully. But the Roman officer has seen! 'I said no drink for that man,' he storms. The carpenter leaves Ben Hur with the cup and rises to look at the officer. Still we cannot see the man's face, but we watch as the Roman officer gazes at him. The power of the Carpenter is revealed. The Roman shows amazement, then shame. He says no more, but turns away, emptied of his venom. But later we will see the men without shame crucifying the Carpenter.

The whole scene moved me immensely. I felt – and this was before the blow – that I was that wretched man. My sins made me as unattractive to God as the ragged, broken galley slave. I identified with Ben Hur, and I was astonished afresh that Jesus could love that much. He faced Rome – to the death – to give me the water of life. Something of the intensity of his love came over. He passionately desired to save me. My sins did not drive him away. They awoke a yet more passionate determination to come to me.

I hope you are moved by Jesus in the dock. I hope you feel the extravagance, the wild abandon, of his love for you. I weep afresh as I write this chapter. I hope I never speak of this doctrine with dry eyes again.

However, one problem yet remains. It's a problem that lies within us, in our attitude. Terrifying as the law court is, we do not readily relinquish it. We choose not to walk away from it, free, because it offers us something that we really want, that Jesus doesn't give us. It offers us the hope of justifying ourselves; to be justified, found 'not guilty', on our own merits. How we humans long for that!

And why do we wish to justify ourselves? Because the justification Jesus brings is a blow to our pride. We find it humiliating to live on another's charity. It lowers us to admit that we couldn't save ourselves. We'd rather stay in the law court, pleading our case. Who knows, we might win someday. . . .

But that's no way to talk! At this rate, you'll never leave! Don't be a fool! The drowning man doesn't refuse the 'charity' of a lifebelt – or if he does, he drowns.

Make no mistake: many do drown in the law court. Guilt, self-justification, blame and anguish – these can inflict real wounds. Have you ever visited a psychiatric hospital and spoken to patients suffering the most extreme disorders? If so, you will have met with guilt and the others, grown to giant proportions. It is as if they are tangible torturers, striding the wards, wielding their whips. Have you seen the tortured faces? Have you heard their hopeless voices?

I will never forget one such visit. I was a young minister, visiting a member of the church who was in the extremity of mental illness. As I waited for her to be fetched, a man began to speak to me. He had noticed that I was a minister, and launched into a justification of his behaviour in the Second World War. He had, it seems, been an exemplary soldier. However, there had been that matter of the girl in France. Many other soldiers, he told me, had been unfaithful to their wives while on active service. Most were worse than he, he told me. Surely his otherwise good conduct made up for this one lapse.

He told me all this, and I never asked a single question! Out it all poured – the guilt of a sin committed a generation before. The court had been trying the case since then, and, judging by his intensity, it was still frantically hearing the same old evidence. All those years had passed, yet he was still hoping to justify himself. He poured it all out to me, his eyes begging me to find him innocent.

The poor man was a patient in that sad ward. Guilt and self-justification had tortured him nearly to the point of complete destruction. His human soul had almost disappeared beneath the weight of compulsive legalities and misery. I tried to explain to him a better way than self-justification, but he was no longer able to choose to rest his case. Make no mistake: the time to resolve this is now.

Jesus had something to say about justification. It isn't just we who have the law court – they had it then too. Jesus told a parable 'to some who trusted in themselves that they were righteous, and despised others' (Lk 18:9). They thought that they could win the case, come out of the trial innocent, 'righteous'. Others couldn't, and they despised them for it.

Here is the parable:

> Two men went up to the temple to pray, one a Pharisee and the other a tax collector. The Pharisee stood and prayed thus with himself, 'God, I thank You that I am not like other men – extortioners, unjust, adulterers, or even as this tax collector. I fast twice a week; I give tithes of all that I possess.' And the tax collector, standing afar off, would not so much as raise his eyes to heaven, but beat his breast, saying, 'God, be merciful to me a sinner!' I tell you, this man went down to his house justified rather than the other; for everyone who exalts himself will be humbled, and he who humbles himself will be exalted (Lk 18:10–14).

When I first read this, I was outraged at the Pharisee. What arrogance! What pride! More recently, I begin to fear that I am all too like him. He knew that he lived a decent life, better than many, and he had the grace to thank God for it. It's thanks to God – not me – he declared, that I am a good person.

However, he went terribly wrong. Where did he go wrong? The parable is for those who 'trusted in themselves that they were righteous'. Yes, we should thank God for the goodness we have, but we must not think that it justifies us. The Pharisee may have been more moral than the tax collector, but he was still a sinner, guilty in the law court. There is not a great deal of difference from God's viewpoint. Sin is sin, big or small. God's attitude to sin is unequivocal: 'For You are not a God who takes pleasure in wickedness, nor shall evil dwell with You. The boastful shall not stand in Your sight; You hate all workers of iniquity. You shall destroy those who speak falsehood; the Lord abhors the bloodthirsty and deceitful man' (Ps 5:4–6).

There could hardly be a clearer statement: God cannot abide sin. And neither (apart from his justification) can he abide the sinner: 'You hate all workers of iniquity.' In the face of this, what point is there to the plea: I'm better than others? Perhaps you are. Perhaps the Pharisee was. So what? God hates all workers of iniquity.

It seems there are degrees of punishment in hell (Mt 10:15), but is that what we seek – slightly less torment than others have? Surely there is something better than that!

Evidently the Pharisee was not, in his own opinion, a sinner at all. His law court found him 'not guilty'. But in this he was dreadfully mistaken; fearfully, disastrously mistaken. Far more mistaken than any of us can afford to be.

The tax collector knew that he could never be justified by his own life, and that he needed to be justified by God, otherwise he would never leave the law court a free man. He knew he needed mercy – not justice – and he got it.

Let's see how. First, he found himself guilty. No plea, no excuses, no extenuating circumstances. Just plain 'guilty'. As the Bible says, 'If we would judge ourselves, we would not be judged' (1 Cor 11:31). 'The tax collector, standing afar off, would not so much as raise his eyes to heaven, but beat his breast, saying, "God, be merciful to me a sinner!"'

Notice that he didn't merely ask God for some help and try to combine his own goodness with what God gave. It wasn't a team effort. He knew that justice found him guilty, and all his hope was in mercy.

God's mercy, so dearly bought for us by Jesus, is free. The tax collector stood in the temple, where he saw the various God-given symbols that foreshadowed Christ's death for us. However unclear in their details, he knew they spelled 'mercy'. Mercy was his only hope, and he pleaded for it humbly; the helpless beggar pleading for charity. And he received it, fully and freely: 'I tell you, this man went down to his house justified rather than the other; for everyone who exalts himself will be humbled, and he who humbles himself will be exalted.'

It's good to carry the law court around within us, and we should always do so. But remember, it's the law court with Jesus in the dock. It's the court where we guilty ones find mercy, because he took our guilt.

Maybe that's what Christ's Bride means by: 'A bundle of myrrh is my beloved to me, that lies all night between my breasts' (Song 1:13). Myrrh, the burial herb, signifies Christ's death. All through the 'night' of this life – before eternal day dawns – she carries this beloved death. It is kept in her very bosom, close to her heart: 'Always carrying about in the body the dying of the Lord Jesus, that the life of Jesus also may be manifested in our body' (2 Cor 4:10). This fragrant herb is a continual reminder that Christ died for me! I am justified by his blood.

Paul 'determined not to know anything among you except Jesus Christ and Him crucified' (1 Cor 2:2). He did so, because he knew himself 'justified freely by His grace through the redemption that is in Christ Jesus' (Rom 3:24). The cross of Christ is always relevant. All 'fall short of the glory of God' (Rom 3:23), and need mercy all the time.

So let's keep this law court with us. Let's see Jesus in the dock, on the cross. Let's remember that we are not good enough in ourselves.

To think like this changes us. Gone are the self-justification, self-righteousness and accompanying condemnation of others. Instead, there is gratitude, joy, praise and freedom. The law court is no longer the vicious circle of obsessive thoughts. It is renamed 'Calvary', the place of Christ's glory and our gladness.

This is not just a matter of inward thoughts. People are always asking the suddenly single about what happened. We are tempted to answer in a way that justifies us and we try to satisfy the inward court by our outward answers. If we convince our friends that we are completely innocent, we feel better inside – for the time being.

But it does no good. To start with it locks us further into the inner law court. Then it makes us need others' good opinions for our well-being, and this is disastrous. 'You will keep him in perfect peace, whose mind is stayed on You, because he trusts in You' (Is 26:3). Our peace comes from relying on God, not the opinions of

others. 'Woe to you when all men speak well of you,'
said Jesus (Lk 6:26).

It is far better to imitate Jesus, and refrain from self-
justification. 'He was oppressed and He was afflicted,
yet He opened not His mouth' (Is 53:7). There is great
dignity in such a silence. By all means let us talk about
what happened. We may even wish to tell a very close
friend everything. But we mustn't select the facts to put
ourselves in the best light. God is our Judge, not our
friends. We keep our dignity when we refuse to blurt out
our self-justification.

So, you must no longer blame your 'ex'. You don't
need to. Your innocence does not depend on Lee's guilt.
God alone knows the balance of guilt and innocence. He
knows who was to blame and where. He knows 'whose
fault' it was.

Your law court can have a much-needed recess. You
have dropped your suit against Lee, and you pray Lee
will receive mercy, as you have. You do not wish to
condemn, nor do you desire to establish your own innocence. God knows where you have been wrong, and you
know it is paid for. Your tortured mind can rest in peace.
Court is adjourned.

6

Lovable?

How do we express our need to be loved? Being loved is the kind of thing we take for granted. It affects everything we do, and yet we may not even think about it. It is the kind of thing that we do not notice – until it is gone.

Solomon says:

> Two are better than one, because they have a good reward for their labor. For if they fall, one will lift up his companion. But woe to him who is alone when he falls, for he has no one to help him up. Again, if two lie down together, they will keep warm; but how can one be warm alone? Though one may be overpowered by another, two can withstand him. And a threefold cord is not quickly broken (Eccl 4:9–12).

Yes, this says something of it. 'They have a good reward for their labor.' You did something, and it was good, but it wasn't satisfying until you told the one you love. You didn't have the 'good reward' until your love could enjoy it too.

And yes, you were there to 'lift up' one another. Love, not muscles, lifts you up. But now, 'Woe to him who is alone when he falls, for he has no one to help him.' Woe to him who is alone! But you are alone. No one, it seems, really loves you.

'Again, if two lie down together, they will keep warm; but how can one be warm alone?' He isn't talking about mere physical warmth, is he? This is not something a hot water bottle can cure, is it? There is a warmth that goes into the very soul, and it is nothing to do with the temperature of the room. Ah, but you knew all about that, didn't you? Once.

There is no loneliness like the loneliness of a bed. Once, you were used to the warmth of loving and being loved. Today, even if you can keep busy and occupied during the day, there is no escape because eventually you must go to bed. Alone. There is something about the emptiness of a bed that only the suddenly single know about.

We could talk about your friends. No doubt you have many, and they love you. We could talk about your family, who love you too. Probably that means more: they know you in a different way. Yes, we could talk. But what good is the talk? The fact is, nobody knew you like the one who is gone. And, against that fact, all the other facts – friends, family – cannot turn the scales.

You married someone who chose you in a unique way. Lee loved you, knew you, gave up all the rest for you. It is not just that you aren't loved. Lee's going says that you're not lovable. That's how it feels, doesn't it? If your love could not love you any more, then who out of those who really know you could?

And when you remember the things your love said – and you keep remembering them all the time – the point is clearer still: 'I don't love you. I never loved you. Living with you is so dull – I need to *live* my life. You're such a selfish, unattractive person, so taken up with your own petty things. You'll never change . . . ' And all the rest. Did they really mean it? Was it really true? You don't know. But the point is, those things have been said, and they all add up to one thing: Who could love me?

You need to be loved. You are not loved. You are not, it seems, lovable. How will you cope with it?

Who could love me?

Perhaps you were impatient with those who would go on about not being loved. 'No one loves me,' they used to moan. 'No one could.' 'Of course they do,' you insisted, wondering how to convince them. If only they would talk less about love, and just love people, their problems might disappear. Or so you sometimes thought. Anyway, you kept on assuring them of their loveliness. But maybe you found it all a bit of an effort.

Now you're sounding just like them. The fact is, Lee's going changed everything. When Lee went, the foundations of your life went as well. We don't notice foundations until they are gone. When foundations collapse, everything else crumbles too. Being loved is foundational.

Of course, lots of people love you and they have taken pains to assure you that you are loved. 'You don't know how much we love you,' they say. They're right – you don't know. You appreciate what they say – they are very kind – but the person who knew you and loved you the most has gone. Your love went, not loving you. Lee did not think you lovable. And that's one person who ought to know.

Now, how are you going to deal with that? Because something must be done. We have a defence mechanism, a survival instinct, and we must do something – anything – to cope with this new 'fact'. What attitude can the unlovely hold?

A few choices suggest themselves. You could become

hard and bitter. Life has shot you in the back, and you are under no illusions. You know what life is really like. You see a young couple in love, and you smile bitterly. If only they knew what you know, they wouldn't be planning their future so happily. 'Don't talk to me about love,' you say. 'I've been there, seen it all. They say one thing, mean another. You can't trust people.'

You might call this being 'realistic', but a better word would be 'cynical'. It really is no better than suicide. Don't choose this option, because it causes you to die so far as being a warm, loving human being is concerned. God has something far better.

Another way out is to become sentimental. You could become a tearful sponge, soaking up love and attention from others. This is not as difficult as it sounds. Have you found yourself crying when loving folk are sympathising with you? What happened then? They sympathised all the more, didn't they? You became the centre of attention. Arms were flung round you. Loving things were said to you.

For the moment, you felt much better, but later the feeling wore off, and you started to think how it wouldn't be hard to get that feeling back. You could break down again. There would be no hypocrisy in that, because you really do feel awful. And then you would be the centre of attention again. Have you not felt tempted to go back again and again for this relief?

But, of course, 'temptation' is the right word, because this is a kind of emotional blackmail. They have to pour love out to you. How could they refuse, with the state you are in? Soon, some of them will be avoiding you, because they will sense that you are manipulating their emotions for your own ends. Others will feel that they have to be there for you, but you know that you are using – abusing – them. You will have turned into a sponge – soft and spineless and, to tell the truth, not very lovable. This isn't God's way either.

Another option is to become drab. The drab person knows they're not lovable. They may not be cynical, they don't manipulate love from others, but they have given up. So they reconcile themselves to being unlovable.

Being unlovable is not without its consolations. You need not make special efforts to look lovely, and this saves time and energy. You can indulge yourself in the unhealthy, the fattening, because after all you deserve a treat! But this turns into an endless series of treats. Why care what you look like? Why deny yourself when nobody really cares anyway? If you're drab, you won't be disappointed. You don't expect to be loved, and you get no nasty shocks.

Of course, this is another kind of suicide. It is to amputate such a very human part of ourselves – the longing for love – in order to create a pain-free existence. But God doesn't want us crippled or dead; he wants us gloriously, radiantly alive.

Have you felt the pull of these temptations? I have; all of them. They are mutually exclusive, but I've felt them at the same time. It was as if they took turns with me. They may not sound very tempting to some, but I found them very tempting indeed. Resisting them was impossible, unless something better could be found.

The new me

Did your 'ex' tell you that you needed to change? Was it on the way out of the door, or was it: 'You'll never change!'? At the time you swore you'd change, whatever that meant. Actually, you may not have been at all sure what it did mean. How, exactly, were you meant to change? Or rather, into what?

Perhaps, looking back, you see that your love didn't want you to change; Lee wanted to change you, for another love. It wasn't a 'new you' that was wanted; it was a new lover altogether. Maybe you made desperate efforts to change, before it was too late. And if you did, perhaps you found to your mystification that it wasn't making any difference at all.

Now your love has gone, it is you who wants to change. When I was trying to recover from sudden singlehood, I found I wanted to be different. I don't mean becoming a better person – although there was that too – but just being different. It was good to dress differently, adopt different habits. If I found that I spoke differently, or went to different places, I was pleased. I ate different foods and began to like things I hadn't liked before.

These weren't startling differences, and most people wouldn't have noticed most of them, but I noticed. And I was glad. I wanted to be a 'new me'.

Have you noticed anything like this in yourself? Perhaps you've been surprised by it, but there's nothing strange about it, when you stop and think. It's an expression of hope. The old life has been suddenly destroyed with such complete desolation that it can't be rebuilt. So hope lies in a new life, and these small, outward changes are a sign, hopefully, that a new life is coming.

If this were all – new tastes, new habits, new appearance – then the 'new me' would be a cruel hoax. Holding out hope of new life, it would deliver nothing except new externals. We cannot renew ourselves, but we can be renewed. In fact, we already have been, and now is a good time to recognise it.

George MacDonald's classic *Lilith* is a favourite book

of mine. In it, the hero finds himself in a strange land that parallels our own world. There he sees the mysterious Mr Raven pluck a worm out of the ground and flick it into the air. Immediately, it turns into a glorious butterfly, which glows with its own light. The ugly, the prosaic, has become beautiful and magnificent. Our hero touches this wonderful butterfly – grown now as large as a kite – and it dies instantly. Its brightness is quenched.

Our hero has seen the miracle of resurrection, but he sees that he lacks this true life in himself. He needs to become a 'new man'. This miracle is indeed offered him, but it does not come easily. First, he must die to the old life. He is shown a vast chamber, where sleepers rest, frozen, on icy beds, and await resurrection. It is too eerie and ghostly for him, so he flees, but must find another path to death and thus to resurrection.

For me, this classic fantasy brings the miracle of resurrection into a fresh light. It is all around us, in nature, in the world God has made. It is so vast! We must not miss it by expecting something less glorious.

Now, while you are looking for the 'new you', it is a good time to see who the 'new you' really is. How is this connected with the misery of being unlovely? It lies in this: God made us lovely by a spiritual resurrection. Everything else we have looked at – God's everlasting love for us, his control of the universe, his justification of us – all these are outside us. Their centre is heaven. But the spiritual resurrection, the new birth, actually changes us. We are different in our very natures. We are increasingly transformed: 'But we all, with unveiled face, beholding as in a mirror the glory of the Lord, are being transformed into the same image from glory to glory, just as by the Spirit of the Lord' (2 Cor 3:18).

Have you ever thought that you are the only person

who can't see you? How do you look to others? You
don't know. You see yourself when you look in the
mirror, but even then you don't see the real you. It's not
you as you normally are; it is you as you look when
you're looking in the mirror. If you could only see yourself through someone else's eyes! But perhaps you can!

The Bible is God's book, which is like a mirror: 'For if
anyone is a hearer of the word and not a doer, he is like
a man observing his natural face in a mirror' (Jas 1:23).
But this mirror shows us ourselves from God's point of
view. Look at the Bible and see yourself.

What is the cure to feeling unlovely? It is to look at
yourself in the mirror of the word. See there the lovely
being you have become. And, as you look, be healed. If
we could really see how lovely the new birth has made
us, we could never feel unlovely.

God's love makes us lovable

'The Lord takes pleasure in His people; He will beautify
the humble with salvation' (Ps 149:4). This is a remarkable verse, and we should read it with care and attention. Who are 'the humble'? They are those who receive
'salvation', because only humble people can be saved by
Christ. The proud are too busy saving themselves. These
humble, saved people are 'His people'.

God says two things about 'His people'. The first is
that they are beautified. The second is that he takes
pleasure in them. This makes sense. If we have made
something beautiful, it gives us pleasure to enjoy it. And
if we plan to enjoy something, we like to make it beautiful first. First we decorate a room, then we enjoy being
in it. Since God plans to enjoy us, it makes sense that he
decorates – beautifies – us first.

But although this verse makes sense, we still find it astonishing. 'God takes pleasure in me? He has beautified me?' I find this so amazing that I can never become used to it. Whenever I see it, it is as if it has come afresh to me for the first time. It seems so impossible. God looks at me and sees me as beautiful. The fact is, I can never get used to being thought lovely by God. And becoming suddenly single makes it all the harder. If my love, who knew me best, stopped loving me, then how can God love me still, for he knows me even better? If I fell below Lee's standards, surely I must fall beneath his!

The truth is, however, that God has done something truly extraordinary to us. He has renewed us; we are born again. And *that* is why we are lovely.

I find myself going to old stories to feel the wonder of what the Bible says. There is the old fairy story of *Beauty and the Beast*, for instance. There the repulsive Beast eventually becomes loved by Beauty, and as soon as this happens, he is transformed into a handsome prince. He becomes lovely, but he had to be loved first. Another fairy story has the ugly frog turning into a handsome prince, but only when the beautiful princess kisses him first.

Jesus made us lovely by kissing us while we were still ugly.

Few biblical expressions are so commonly used as 'born again'. But I think we use it without really seeing the vast miracle it represents. This is a very good time to look afresh at what we 'born-again' Christians now are. For me, the shock of feeling unlovely, and the instinct to be a 'new man', met in the doctrine of the new birth.

The new birth

Can you remember when you first trusted Christ? It doesn't matter, so long as now, with all your faults and imperfections, your trust is in him. Faith is something that never ages. As you reaffirm your faith in him now, it is like the first time all over again. Join me now in surrendering yourself to Christ afresh. Let's relive that first moment.

What hesitant, stumbling words did we use then? 'Lord Jesus, I put my trust in you. All the sins I've committed, the wrong things I've done, and been . . . Please forgive me. Thank you for taking my sin on the cross. From now on, please help me to follow you, obey you, and be yours for ever.' Then we paused. It seemed such an inadequate prayer. Would God hear these feeble words? Could he read our hearts, and find the confused longing that lay in them?

We couldn't see that this difficult moment was really a supernatural birth. The past months had been a bewildering time. Fear and longing, uncertainty and insight, guilt and desire – all these had struggled within us. But to God, these months had been the pregnancy that precedes the long-awaited birth. People expect problems in pregnancy, and the birth process can be very painful. But all that is natural and normal. We accept it because of our eagerness to see the longed-for child.

As our mumbled prayer tailed off into silence, there was rejoicing in heaven over a sinner repenting. Sadly, we couldn't hear the celebration, but some faint echo touched our hearts. We felt that perhaps something momentous had occurred. How unaware we were of the glory of that moment; of the transformation that had occurred; of the breathtaking glory. We became sons of God: 'For you are all sons of God through faith in Christ Jesus' (Gal 3:26). In us, as in the new-born baby, a discerning eye could see the family likeness. And God has a very discerning eye.

How could this amazing miracle possibly have happened? As parents give something of themselves in the forming of their child, so it is with God. That something of the parents guarantees the family likeness of the child, and so it is with God, our Father. He sees the family likeness in us.

Christians are 'born of the Spirit' (Jn 3:8). The Holy Spirit – the third Person of the Trinity – enters us. He is God. And by his miraculous entry, an unimaginable glory takes place. Inglorious men and women are reborn, now in incandescent loveliness.

The Spirit who enters us, remains with us: 'Do you not know that you are the temple of God and that the Spirit of God dwells in you?' (1 Cor 3:16). In the Old Testament, the temple was where God always was (although he might appear somewhere else temporarily). In this temple, God appeared in indescribable glory; elsewhere only discerning eyes might see him. Now, we are told, it is we who are the temple; we are his permanent, glorious, earthly dwelling.

'Love has been perfected among us in this: that we may have boldness in the day of judgment; because as He is, so are we in this world' (1 Jn 4:17). We believers are 'as He is'; we are like him.

Clearly we cannot be like God in every way. We can never be the Creator, nor all-powerful, nor sovereign, because only God is these things, and we shall always be his creations, looking to him, living by him and for him. Nor are we perfectly like him. So in what ways *are* we like him?

Here are the three main ways. They reveal a three-dimensional picture of you that is very lovely. Look hard at the picture. You are more splendid than even vanity could imagine.

The family likeness

1. *Holiness*

'You put on the new man which was created according to God, in true righteousness and holiness' (Eph 4:24). What was new about the 'new man'? True righteousness and holiness. I remember asking a newly converted girl what her first week as a Christian had been like. She had had an amazing first week. She had been staggered to find that she loved everyone! And what joy! – it was amazing. But it wasn't so very amazing because it was the family likeness.

She had received the Spirit, whose fruit is 'love, joy, peace, longsuffering, kindness, goodness, faithfulness, gentleness, self-control' (Gal 5:22–23). No wonder these things were active in her new life. Finding this new nature is quite a shock – a very pleasant shock – for an adult convert.

We might be amazed at how rarely we feel we have these qualities – we wish we were better people – but the wonder is that we have them as much as we do. It is the miracle of the new birth, fighting against the other forces in our lives. If we could only look dispassionately at ourselves, we would see. We would see that Christlike patterns are at work in us. Try to remember what you used to be like. Can't you see that you are changed?

It is our fault that we are not better than we are, but it is the miracle of the new birth that we are as good as we are. This is nothing to boast of. We must thank God who fathered us, and we must take care not to overlook the beautiful family likeness or deny the miracle of sonship.

God's seed in us cannot fail to produce the family likeness. 'Whoever has been born of God does not sin, for

His seed remains in him; and he cannot sin, because he has been born of God' (1 Jn 3:9). This is not to say that we are already perfect, for other forces wrestle with the family likeness – the world, the flesh and the devil. But the true believer, for all his imperfections, is marked by the fact that he displays a God-given holiness of life. It is already there in the new believer, the baby, but it grows as the believer nears spiritual manhood. Whatever new experiences of the Spirit are yet to come, the Spirit himself is already there. And his influence is growing.

Have you ever found, on occasion, that you couldn't sin; that you – or actually a force within you – really wanted to sin, but you couldn't? The longing to sin was overwhelming, and you felt so bad about that, but in the end you didn't; something within you couldn't. 'His seed remains in him; and he cannot sin.' If only this were always the case!

This holy nature is very beautiful to God. It is said of Christ: 'You have loved righteousness and hated lawlessness' (Heb 1:9). Ask what he really likes and he will tell you: 'Righteousness.' It may not be what everyone likes, but Jesus loves it, and the righteous are lovely to him.

2. Knowledge

'You . . . have put on the new man who is renewed in knowledge according to the image of Him who created him' (Col 3:10). Here is another feature of the family likeness. We know.

What do we know? We may not think we know much. Indeed, in the throes of misery, we feel we know nothing at all. But we know things unknown to the wisest, most knowledgeable scholar. 'And this is eternal life, that they may know You, the only true God, and Jesus Christ whom You have sent' (Jn 17:3). Knowledge is the mark of the new life – we know God.

In the course of studying theology at universities, I have met many learned and widely-read scholars. I am so grateful for their example of thorough research and consistent thinking, and I wish I could learn all that they know, but some lacked what the simplest believer enjoys: the knowledge of God.

How sad to see the scholar struggle as he tries to make sense of the mysteries of the faith. He is sincere. He is clever. He is working hard. But he cannot make sense of it because for all his learning, he only knows *about* God. But the simplest believer, who thinks he knows nothing, knows God. The believing scholar has a knowledge of God too. He loves his books, but he also knows God by the Spirit.

Perhaps Christ means this in the Song of Solomon, when he tells us: 'Behold, you are fair, my love! Behold, you are fair! You have dove's eyes' (Song 1:15). 'Dove's eyes'! The dove often represents the Spirit in the Bible. And to have the Spirit's eyes must mean that we know things by the Spirit. These spiritual eyes make us very attractive to God.

Imagine it: whereas God sees everyone, he sees them ignoring him, or searching for him. They are looking around, looking this way and that, but their eyes don't fix on him. It is as if he isn't there. How strange, since God fills all things! But there are others. These are God's dear children. They too look around, and they *can* see. Their eyes settle on God, and they know him and love him. You can imagine how attractive this must make us. We can see him and we love him. He appreciates that.

Sometimes I ask myself how I survived sudden single-hood. The simple answer is: God. But how did God do

91

it? I am fairly sure he did it through doctrine – at least doctrine seemed to play the largest part. And it was this that gave me the urgency to write this book. I know that doctrine is not very popular, and people think that it is dull and lifeless. However, it is anything but. For me, it was life-giving. 'Lord, to whom shall we go? You have the words of eternal life' (Jn 6:68).

These 'doctrines' are truths that God has given. So how could they ever be unpopular? Perhaps it is because we in the twentieth century are more interested in how we feel than in truth. But the more we concentrate on what we feel, the more difficulties our feelings give us. However, if we love the doctrine because it is true, then feelings come into line. At any rate, the agony is less than it might have been. At least this is my experience.

People have been surprised to see me recover from sudden singlehood so quickly. I would like to see you recover even faster. Hence the doctrines.

How do we know a doctrine? A believer knows it in a special way. He knows it is true and, what's more, he can feel the goodness in it. It is true in the same way as it is true that Australia exists. But it is more than that. It feels like Australia exists *and* we are off on holiday there.

We know it, because the Spirit has convinced us of the utter and unique truth of the Bible. The Bible is God's word. It is as true as God, just as I am as truthful as the things I say. But the words of the Bible are like bricks, and God's people, relying on the Spirit's help, have built doctrines from these bricks. The church is not always right – indeed we have had to correct mistakes from our past – but we can feel confident of the central doctrines.

Not that we simply take these doctrines, ready made, from the hands of our spiritual fathers. They have given us their blueprints, and we rebuild the doctrines ourselves, from the Scriptures. Once we have done that, we can feel confident. We are like a builder, who looks with satisfaction at the house he has built. He knows that the work is properly done, and reliable. He knows, because he did it himself. So, we too can hold our doctrines, knowing that they are built securely from the verses of the Bible.

When I became suddenly single, it wasn't a good time to build doctrines, but I found that I had doctrines already built. Some of them never tasted so good as they did then. This book contains all the main ones that helped me.

But there is a knowledge that is much harder to express. How can we explain what knowing God feels like? Like all really important things – love, joy and the rest – it 'passes knowledge'; it is inexpressible, but we know it.

We have a set of beliefs, but God is larger than that. We have spiritual experiences, but God is bigger than them all. We have standards, a way of life, but God is above them. He is in all these things, but none of them is him. Yet, great as he is, we know him, although we can't explain it.

You know him, and it may seem at this time that this is all you know, but this is part of the 'new you', and it is very beautiful in God's eyes.

3. Victory

Now, more than ever, you feel powerless. You feel anything but victorious. You feel as if life has you in its jaws and is shaking you, like a dog shakes a rat. You may feel like Job, whose best hope was that he would die soon. But it has not always been so. Nor will it be so in the future.

Jesus left his church much to do. He said:

All authority has been given to Me in heaven and on earth.
Go therefore and make disciples of all the nations, baptizing
them in the name of the Father and of the Son and of the
Holy Spirit, teaching them to observe all things that I have
commanded you; and lo, I am with you always, even to the
end of the age (Mt 28:18–20).

His death for sinners is done. That part of the job was
finished, without our help, just as his resurrection and
ascension were too. There, in heaven, all authority on
earth is his, and he is with us always; with us in authority, so that we can finish the job of discipling the nations.
We have the mighty word, and the Spirit is given, con-
victing sinners and providing works of power.

So, be honest. Haven't you been used by God? Even
now you might be, although it's difficult to imagine. You
may feel an utter failure at the moment, thinking that
you ought to be coping with the crisis a lot better. I felt
I should have been much more spiritual in it all. But for
all that, this is a time of unparalleled awfulness, and you
are doing much better than you might. People are
watching. Perhaps they are learning something.

Think back to the past and what you have done for
your God. It may not seem much, but it was something,
and God may think more of it than you do. In any case,
you are part of the team. You and Jesus, and the rest of
us, are working together. There is a special closeness in
a team. We feel we are 'in it together'. There is a close
sense of brotherhood, of camaraderie, 'for we are God's
fellow workers' (1 Cor 3:9).

Perhaps it is like being a youngster who is called to
play in a team because a grown-up is injured. He is
smaller, younger, than everyone else and he doesn't feel

worthy; perhaps the grown-ups are his heroes. He does less than anyone else and makes more mistakes, but do you think it is held against him? Of course not! After the game, the other members all tell him how good he was, and treat him as part of the team.

We have been called onto the team by our hero, Jesus, the Captain. There are some famous names in the team, great leaders of the church, and we may feel like the youngster, the least talented. And who cares if we are? Jesus knows our gifting, and will say: 'Well done!' We are in the same team. We have a special bond.

The heroes of the Bible were those who believed God and had a go. They weren't much to start with, but later they became the great heroes we remember. They weren't born heroes; their power came from trusting God: 'For whatever is born of God overcomes the world. And this is the victory that has overcome the world – our faith. Who is he who overcomes the world, but he who believes that Jesus is the Son of God?' (1 Jn 5:4–5).

This is not a good time to be told to be more victorious – it is probably the last thing you can cope with – but maybe it's good to hear that you are victorious. Your faith, in the past, has achieved victories, and it will do again.

Some years ago I had set time aside for prayer and fasting, and I had borrowed a friend's empty house for this purpose. There, undisturbed, I could pray and seek God. Times of prayer and fasting can be so wonderful, but on that occasion I felt anything but wonderful. I felt anything but victorious. I felt an utter failure.

This kind of despair can be paralysing. As I tried to pray, I sensed that I was to go up to the top floor and pray there. I did so, and perhaps my faith climbed a little as I went up the stairs. At the top I knelt down, then a vivid picture came to mind. I felt that I was an athlete, surrounded by thousands of spectators, the 'great cloud of witnesses' Paul speaks about.

It seemed to me that I might be muddy and sweaty; I might be puffed out and exhausted; I might ache and be bruised – but that was all right. Athletes get like that. But the contest wasn't over, and the spectators were shouting for me: 'Go on!' This was no time to give in. I had to pull myself together, and see about fighting on.

It seemed to me that the 'great cloud of witnesses', saints of past ages, would sympathise with me. They too were bruised and discouraged, they too felt failures, but they kept going.

You keep going too. You were picked by Jesus for his team. The new birth fits you for the part he has planned for you. You have won before and you will win again. Now keep going. Don't think that all that mud and bruising makes you unlovely. God loves your faith and the victories he sees faith winning. He loves his likeness in you. He loves your righteousness, although it is not as yet complete. He loves your knowledge of him, even though it is still growing.

He loves *you*. Keep looking in the mirror of the word, because if you could see yourself as he sees you, you'd see how lovely you are. You are a 'new you'. You are lovely.

Now how will you respond to that?

7

Pain

I suppose I must have lived an easy life because looking
back not much has happened to me that was bad – really
bad, I mean. I would never have actually said: 'I don't
know what pain really is,' but I think that was the truth.
I didn't really know.

That was back then, of course.

How about you? Has this been a bit of a revelation to
you too? There were times when I couldn't believe how
much it hurt. I didn't think it was possible to be in so
much pain. And I couldn't see it ever ending.

You understand me all too well, I imagine.

Pain is such a relative thing. A child seems to experience excruciating pain over something trivial. A balloon
bursts, and the child's world falls apart. The solution is
equally trivial: another balloon, and all is well. Two new
balloons would spell ecstasy. For a while. Then the
whole business of balloons is forgotten.

When a child is in pain, you hold him, and eventually
the pain subsides. Who would expect a child to cry for
hours? Or days? Or weeks?

Weeks! You would be very pleased to hear that the
pain would be over in mere weeks, or even months. But
you fear it will be years. Or never.

If only you were a child, with a child's pain! You would cry yourself to sleep, and tomorrow morning it would be gone. If only a balloon or two would cure it. But of course it is not like that.

It is not like bodily pain either. A burn or an external wound causes pain, and toothache is worse, because it seems to get inside you. And what about migraines? They seem to take root right in your mind. But, painful as these are, they are only physical. Becoming suddenly single went into your very soul. It bypassed the body where, theoretically, pain relief can be had. It settled in your soul, your 'you'. There is no escape from that.

It is like having a tooth out, except that it is a part of 'you' that is out, and you can't live without it.

It is like being annihilated, except that you're still alive to feel it.

It is a death, but not a quick death. Not a death that is over with. It is a death that lingers on and on.

It is like drowning, but you don't actually drown. You plead with God, as Job did, to finish you off, but he won't. You reach up a hand for his hand, but he doesn't pull you out. There is no rescue, no lifebelt. You just keep on drowning.

This kind of pain underlies everything. You can be cheerful, even seem to forget, but it is really there all the time. And in a second you step out of the light into pitch darkness. One moment you are smiling at what your friend says, the next the darkness has closed in on you again.

No one can live with that sort of pain. You know you must do something to cope with it. But what *can* you do?

Pain-killers

You need pain-killers. After all, the pain must be killed.
Better to kill the pain than the pain kill you.

Alcohol

Could this be the balloon which will cheer you up?

In an ideal world, of course, such a drug would not be
needed, but since the Fall this hasn't been an ideal
world. So the Bible acknowledges the anaesthetising
aspect of alcohol: 'Give strong drink to him who is per-
ishing, and wine to those who are bitter of heart. Let
him drink and forget his poverty, and remember his
misery no more' (Prov 31:6–7).

God knows that life will have its bitterness, and
alcohol might lessen the pain – for a while. But it won't
cure. Isn't that the temptation? If one balloon doesn't
stop the crying, why not two, or three, or four? And
then, when the crying starts again, more balloons. . . .
This is not a good time to acquire more problems! 'Give
strong drink to him,' says God, but he also warns us:
'Wine is a mocker, strong drink is a brawler, and
whoever is led astray by it is not wise' (Prov 20:1). Don't
be led astray! It *isn't* a balloon – it won't kill the pain.
Much the same can be said for medicinal pain-killers.

Exercise

Yes, sudden singlehood can wreak havoc with your body,
but it works the other way round too: 'Bodily exercise
profits a little' (1 Tim 4:8). God has built pleasure into
healthy exercise. A strenuous walk, a session of aerobics,
a body in a healthy condition – these produce an inner
well-being that goes into the balance against the awful
pain. They cannot, of course, outweigh the pain, but they

do help. You feel a little more fit, a little less fat. The 'new me' feels in rather better shape than the old me did. And in the worst bouts of pain, there is a release in physical exercise, the harder the better. The soul is in darkness, but the body feels exhilarated by a fierce sprint.

There is another benefit to this exercise: it will help you keep a check on your body. If you are not eating or sleeping as you should, you will know it when you try exercising. It will warn you that your body is dangerously weak!

Someone needs to keep an eye on your body. If you are not used to cooking for yourself, are you getting a balanced diet? Are you eating enough? Are you drinking too much? Are you sleeping properly? If you see a doctor, these are the first things he will ask. When the body feels bad, the whole person feels worse than ever.

I am grateful for the opportunity I had to use a gym through my blackest days. I also played some indoor tennis. I am no good at tennis, but that isn't the point. It was a chance to run around and burn up some energy. Sport – however bad you are at it – is a way to meet new people. I found this very helpful. They didn't know me, and knew nothing of my sudden singlehood. It was good to mix with people who were unaware of my grief, because not knowing about it meant they couldn't be kind, and that made a pleasant change. Sport creates an automatic companionship which is undemanding. This helped me.

You may not have been the 'fitness' type before, but who knows what the 'new you' will be like?

Art

What sort of art do you like? I mean 'art' in the widest sense – books, films, painting, music – whatever moves you. Art is very much a matter of taste. It's up to you what you like.

Judging from the Bible, art is supposed to be a major part of human life. God made the universe with exquisite artistry. I live by the South Downs, near the sea, and if I could describe the things I see, I would be a poet.

Walking is excellent exercise, but if you live near open country, or a park, it is good in another way. Look around you. See that tree, with its golden autumnal leaves shedding to form a golden carpet. Its precise shape is utterly unique, with a dignity and grace that cannot be described. Look away across the gently rolling hills, the warm comfort of the valleys. Here and there a farmhouse sits, as natural as if it had grown there. The trees, the sheep, the flint walls – all seem to form part of a complex pattern, designed by a master artist. God is that master artist. He made it for us, and it does us good to see it.

But man, the crown of creation, is made in God's image. On our own small scale, we too have the power to create. We have created the wonders of today's technological world. Thank God for it – it was God who made us creative.

We also create art. The Bible tells us that art is important. When God ordered a portable worship centre to be built – Moses' Tabernacle – his first requirement was an artist. God told Moses:

> See, I have called by name Bezalel the son of Uri, the son of Hur, of the tribe of Judah. And I have filled him with the Spirit of God, in wisdom, in understanding, in knowledge, and in all manner of workmanship, to design artistic works, to work in gold, in silver, in bronze, in cutting jewels for setting, in carving wood, and to work in all manner of workmanship (Exod 31:2–5).

101

Bezalel was the first person in the Bible of whom it is said he was 'filled with the Spirit'. Later on we find Spirit-filled people working miracles and taking the gospel around the world, but the first Spirit-filled person was an artist. His calling was to create an artistic masterpiece, the Tabernacle.

The Tabernacle was full of prophetic symbols. Christ could be seen in it, in the mercy seat, in the sacrificial altar. It also served the Israelites of the day as their worship centre. I suppose it did not have to be artistic. It could have been merely functional.

'Art is only escapism,' some say. 'You are escaping into your world of books and music.' I have always wondered what is so bad about escaping. Would a prisoner of war feel bad about escaping? Is it better to stay imprisoned? We are not, after all, trying to get away from life. We are trying to survive bitter pain. We want to avoid death in this battle, to live to fight in the next. The prisoner escapes so that he can return home to fight again. Art is an escape that returns us to ordinary life, ennobled.

When I became suddenly single, I wanted to escape the pain, and I was very grateful for art. There is a piece of music – Mahler's 6th Symphony, final movement – which is the saddest piece of music I've ever heard. It's strange that I only want to listen to it when I'm sad myself. . . .

In this piece, there is a sad but hopeful theme that keeps trying to rise, take wing and fly. But as it is leaving the ground, it is smashed to earth with a thunderous blow. The reverberations seem to echo for ages. At last, its strength exhausted, it fades into silence. But just to make sure that it is truly annihilated, it receives one final, devastating blow, and is still. The blows are so heavy that Mahler actually added a sledgehammer and anvil to the orchestra.

The music is terribly beautiful, but also terribly sad. Why is it a comfort? Somehow, what is miserable in real life becomes magnificent in art. The hero has been crushed by unendurable sorrow, and as he sinks, heroic in dignity, your tears flow unbidden. These tears are different from those you cry for yourself. Art lends them a grandeur. And, when the hero fades from view, your grief has been eased, or dignified, and rendered more bearable.

It is dreadfully hard to see your family go, if that is what sudden singlehood has meant for you. It isn't grand, or noble, or beautiful. It is just plain miserable. But when Wotan, in Wagner's 'Ring', says farewell to Brunhilde his daughter, there is grandeur and beauty. His heart is almost breaking, for all his awesome power. He will never see her again. The music is so beautiful that a stone would weep.

This is what art does.

But be warned: art is dangerous too. The art forms carry their own viewpoint, and these aren't usually God's viewpoint. They have the power to influence us subtly. Favourite characters in books and films can voice ungodly ideas. Somehow, the pleasant voice makes the view plausible.

Showing feelings

How fashions change! The Englishman of recent history had to keep the 'stiff upper lip' – it was bad form to show excessive feeling. Before that, the ancient English were very expressive of their feelings. Today, the fashion has changed again. We are told that we must be 'in touch with our feelings', and that the worst thing is to

suppress what we feel. It is better to lose our tempers
than hide our feelings. However, 'a fool vents all his feelings,' the Bible says, 'but a wise man holds them back'
(Prov 29:11).

Which is the Bible way? Well, they are both there.
'Son of man,' said God to Ezekiel, 'behold, I take away
from you the desire of your eyes with one stroke; yet you
shall neither mourn nor weep, nor shall your tears run
down. Sigh in silence, make no mourning for the dead;
bind your turban on your head, and put your sandals on
your feet; do not cover your lips, and do not eat man's
bread of sorrow.' Ezekiel said, 'So I spoke to the people
in the morning, and at evening my wife died; and the
next morning I did as I was commanded' (Ezek
24:16–18).

This is remarkable self-control. It is good to be able
to control our feelings, but, on the other hand, 'Oh,
that my head were waters, and my eyes a fountain of
tears, that I might weep day and night for the slain of
the daughter of my people!' (Jer 9:1). Jesus himself
wept – without apparent restraint – on more than one
occasion.

There is 'a time to weep, and a time to laugh; a time
to mourn, and a time to dance' (Eccl 3:4). There is a
time – and you know that time when it comes.

How different we all are! I don't like showing my feelings publicly, but I do need to express my feelings. I
prefer to do so privately, perhaps crying through a film,
or being deeply moved by a piece of music.

It was good to have a few hand-picked friends to
whom I did want to show my feelings. I could trust them
because they just listened. They didn't try to close down
my feelings, nor to open them up even more.

There isn't going to be a balloon. Whatever helps,

nothing removes this pain. You might as well get used to it – it'll be with you for a while to come.

Knowing Christ in the midst of pain

In our society, although most people don't see the need to follow Christ, they do recognise that religion is good for people – for suffering people, that is. If dreadful things have happened, religion can be a comfort, and people get consolation from God. They assume that this is the point of Christianity.

True, there is consolation in Christ, but that is *not* the point of Christianity. The point of Christianity – of life itself, actually – is the glory of God. It isn't me and my concerns that matter, but him.

People see Christianity through twentieth-century spectacles. The twentieth century has seen the enormous growth of humanism. Humanists believe there is nothing more important than man: it's me who really matters. This attitude is so much in the air around us that we cannot help but pick it up.

We automatically see things from a human perspective. When Christ says, 'Blessed are the peacemakers,' we automatically assume this is referring to peace between man and man. It never occurs to us to think of peace between man and God as well. When we read 1 Corinthians 13, 'Love suffers long and is kind', we think of love between people – not man and God. How strange, when you think that it goes on to say: 'Love believes all things!' Should we really believe all things that people tell us? But if we love God, we do believe all that he says.

So much of the help offered to sufferers is humanistic in nature. Do you feel bad? Then you need to feel good.

That is the human perspective. But what of the divine perspective? God wants us to feel good, but he wants us to *be* good far, far more.

Being good is vital to our long-term happiness. Happiness comes through fulfilment. There is a happiness in physical fulfilment: food, drink, exercise, rest. Higher than that is a happiness from mental fulfilment: having questions answered, knowing understanding. Friendship brings fulfilment too, and so does love. But the highest fulfilment of all is in loving God. We were made for him, and we can only be fully happy if we know him: 'How precious is Your lovingkindness, O God! Therefore the children of men put their trust under the shadow of Your wings. They are abundantly satisfied with the fullness of Your house, and You give them drink from the river of Your pleasures. For with You is the fountain of life; in Your light we see light' (Ps 36:7–9).

There is abundant satisfaction, a river of pleasures, a fountain of life. This happiness surpasses all others. It is eternal, and even in this life it is so much higher than the other pleasures. 'Blessed are those who are persecuted for righteousness' sake, for theirs is the kingdom of heaven' (Mt 5:10). Even the unhappiness of persecution cannot quench the 'blessedness' of God's kingdom.

Yes, the highest happiness is to know God. But to know God, we must be holy: 'Pursue peace with all people, and holiness, without which no one will see the Lord' (Heb 12:14). Why is this? Well, we can't see anything without an image of it within. We see a house because we have its image on our retinas. We 'see' an idea because we have it, as an image, in our thoughts. And we can see God, because we have been changed into his image, but having this 'image' means being holy:

'Blessed are the pure in heart, for they shall see God' (Mt 5:8).

We are told that unbelievers' eyes are 'veiled', and they can't see God's glory. This is not so with believers. We have the Spirit, who enables us to see. How? 'But we all, with unveiled face, beholding as in a mirror the glory of the Lord, are being transformed into the same image from glory to glory, just as by the Spirit of the Lord' (2 Cor 3:18). We see because by the Spirit we 'are being transformed into the same image'. God's glorious image is being reproduced in us.

We are becoming like God in holiness. This likeness to God is 'the new man which was created according to God, in true righteousness and holiness' (Eph 4:24). Therefore, as holiness of life grows, so we 'behold the glory of the Lord' more clearly. And, knowing him, we have found the secret of true happiness. But to know him we must be good. Not *feel* good, *be* good.

And here is the problem with the humanistic solution. It will console us, help us to feel better, but God, who knows best, is improving us, making us better.

So, what about consolation? Yes, there will be consolation, to a degree, but God is more interested in sanctification.

Sanctification

Justification means being found 'not guilty' in God's law court, but it is only half of the story. The other half is sanctification. Sanctification means 'being made holy'. Justification is outward – it is a legal decision in heaven's court – whereas sanctification is inward – we are changed within.

Justification comes first. Without it, we are like criminals on the run, and God is angry with us. Justification

– so expensively bought for us by God – means that we're not wanted by the police any longer. The Holy Spirit comes to us, no longer angry, and with his help we are reformed, sanctified.

Here is another image: we are like a house in a terrible condition which has been condemned as a health hazard. Then God buys it, becoming its legal owner (justification). Then he moves in. He finds it a dreadful mess. First he gets rid of all the rubbish, then he begins to tear the place apart, to make it just right. He rewires, he replaces all the plumbing, he puts in central heating. For a while, the place looks more of a mess than before, but gradually it is being put right. And when he has finished the decorating, it will look fabulous. This is sanctification.

The thing about justification is that it is complete from the start. You can't be more justified than you were at conversion. This is tremendous news, because sanctification is so incomplete, and it can be very disheartening to think how much more sanctification I need! At such times, I remember that I am already fully justified – forgiven, accepted, loved.

The trouble is that God, like the most fastidious decorator, won't be satisfied until he has got us just right. It is not enough for him to clean up the house; he must make it absolutely right. He has the time and resources to do it, but he doesn't have any time to waste.

I started the last paragraph with 'The trouble is . . .' but really I'm glad. And so are you. We really do want to be perfect people, and we are very glad that Christ went to the 'trouble' of dying for us. It's just that sanctification can be very troublesome for us, and in the most painful times we really wish he wouldn't bother.

But he *does* bother. 'Now may the God of peace

Himself sanctify you completely; and may your whole spirit, soul, and body be preserved blameless at the coming of our Lord Jesus Christ' (1 Thess 5:23). This is Paul's prayer. Lest it seem too much to ask, he adds: 'He who calls you is faithful, who also will do it' (v.24). It will happen, because God 'will do it'. It will be completed for me and for you; for every true believer.

What is Christ doing in the midst of our pain?

Christ is not merely consoling us, for it simply would not be in our best interests to do so. The work of our sanctification is just too vast. And since our happiness depends on sanctification, we are glad (with hindsight) that he presses on with that. But of course the house is bound to be torn apart if there is to be new plumbing, wiring, central heating. It simply isn't possible to be sanctified without pain.

For one thing, sanctification involves choosing Christ rather than other, lower pleasures. For such choices to be real, we must be denied other happinesses. There is a direct connection between suffering and forsaking sin: 'Therefore, since Christ suffered for us in the flesh, arm yourselves also with the same mind, for he who has suffered in the flesh has ceased from sin' (1 Pet 4:1).

Job suffered terrible anguish. Satan had accused Job of loving God because of the many earthly pleasures he enjoyed. Now these pleasures were stripped away. What would Job do? 'Then Job arose, tore his robe, and shaved his head; and he fell to the ground and worshiped. And he said: "Naked I came from my mother's womb, and naked shall I return there. The Lord gave, and the Lord has taken away; blessed be the name of the Lord"' (Job 1:20–21).

109

Job's worship, in that awful time, meant so much. The angels must have watched in awe as Job's heart, crushed with misery, blessed the Lord. Worship in times of ease cannot be so precious. A flower can give a beautiful perfume, but to do so in abundance it must be crushed first.

Or, to put the matter another way: we are born again as God's children, but if we are children, God our Father must bring us up properly. A proper upbringing, according to the Bible, means being disciplined:

> And you have forgotten the exhortation which speaks to you as to sons: 'My son, do not despise the chastening of the Lord, nor be discouraged when you are rebuked by Him; for whom the Lord loves He chastens, and scourges every son whom He receives.' If you endure chastening, God deals with you as with sons; for what son is there whom a father does not chasten? But if you are without chastening, of which all have become partakers, then you are illegitimate and not sons. Furthermore, we have had human fathers who corrected us, and we paid them respect. Shall we not much more readily be in subjection to the Father of spirits and live? For they indeed for a few days chastened us as seemed best to them, but He for our profit, that we may be partakers of His holiness. Now no chastening seems to be joyful for the present, but painful; nevertheless, afterward it yields the peaceable fruit of righteousness to those who have been trained by it (Heb 12:5–11).

Look at these words carefully. 'Chastening' and 'correction' are pain words. 'No chastening seems to be joyful for the present, but painful,' it says. It is supposed to hurt. Far from being a sign that God doesn't love us, this pain proves he does. Like a good father, 'As many as I love, I rebuke and chasten. Therefore be zealous and repent' (Rev 3:19).

We will accept this better if we think of how beautiful sanctification is. Think of it now: think of yourself becoming like Christ. Think of all the noble characteristics of Jesus. What do you most admire in him? Is it his love, his gentleness? Is it his power, his firmness? He wouldn't compromise; he died rather than sin. Do you wish you had his peace? Do you envy his popularity with all but the religious hypocrites? Do you want to know the Father as he did?

Sanctification is all this, and more. Furthermore, it is not just for some. All true converts shall attain it, as we saw earlier (1 Thess 5:23–24). Imagine yourself being able to stand in God's presence with no need to confess any shortcoming; you have become sinless. You look at yourself and admire all you see, but without any pride because by now you are more interested in God than yourself anyway. And, as you look at God, you know him as well as he knows you. This is sanctification. If you think this is too good to be true, read 1 John 3:2 – 'Beloved, now we are children of God; and it has not yet been revealed what we shall be, but we know that when He is revealed, we shall be like Him, for we shall see Him as He is.'

So, there will be pain – for you there is pain now – but it is full of purpose and hope:

Most assuredly, I say to you that you will weep and lament, but the world will rejoice; and you will be sorrowful, but your sorrow will be turned into joy. A woman, when she is in labor, has sorrow because her hour has come; but as soon as she has given birth to the child, she no longer remembers the anguish, for joy that a human being has been born into the world. Therefore you now have sorrow; but I will see you again and your heart will rejoice, and your joy no one will take from you (Jn 16:20–22).

Jesus is speaking here of the apostles' anguish during the time between the crucifixion and the resurrection, but it applies to our sorrows too. Yes, there is pain, but it is like the pain a woman feels in childbirth. It produces something that makes it all worthwhile. The mother with the new baby 'no longer remembers the anguish'. She is so glad of the new person before her.

It is the same for you. At the end of the pain there will be a new person to be glad of. It will be you. You will be a new person, because you will be more sanctified. The joy of this more Christlike you makes the pain worth it. This joy, 'no one will take from you'.

Sanctification may seem to take for ever since the process goes on until death, but these few earthly years aren't for ever. 'For ever' is the eternity during which we shall enjoy being sanctified.

Notice he says that if we were not sanctified through pain, then we would be 'illegitimate and not sons'. An Olympic athlete, who carries his country's name and honour, trains hard. He goes through the pain in the gym so that he can receive the glory in the stadium. He doesn't train because he is unfit (he is already a physical masterpiece), but his body is being transformed from glory to glory.

It is the same with us. It is because we are already God's dear children; it is because we are already holy. Job's friends were wrong to attribute his sufferings to sin. But Job, already 'blameless and upright, and one who feared God and shunned evil' (Job 1:1), was even better by the end of the process.

Don't be discouraged that God has to sanctify you. You are most privileged, honoured beyond words, favoured above angels.

Knowing this doesn't lessen the pain, but it does help us bear up beneath it.

With Jesus in the school of pain

'This hurts me more than it hurts you' is the classic line given as a father corrects his child. The child quite frankly doubts it. But in God's case it is undeniably true. 'For it was fitting for Him, for whom are all things and by whom are all things, in bringing many sons to glory, to make the captain of their salvation perfect through sufferings' (Heb 2:10). The same God who disciplines us was himself disciplined (although sinless) by sufferings. He is our captain – our leader – who trod the path ahead of us, and said: 'Follow me.'

The path is pitch dark. Occasionally, in a flash of lightning, you see Christ toiling beside you, otherwise you seem to be alone in the storm. Your cries for help appear to go unheard, drowned out by the thunder. If you bless the Lord, like Job, it is through gritted teeth. You don't hear the crescendo of amazed angels giving 'Amen!' to your muted praise.

Pain is insistent, and clamours for our attention, while truth is quieter, waiting patiently to be noticed. Pain made me ask 'why?'. 'Where are you, Lord?' I cried. 'How can you be close, and not take this pain away? Give me something for the pain!'

It made no sense that the pain remained. Like a child, I wanted the grown-up to 'make it all right' – *now*! I felt God's gentle presence, but that wasn't enough. Like a petulant child who has been denied his own way I lashed out at God: 'If you won't remove this pain, go away! I know you don't love me!' Job speaks of 'the speeches of a desperate one, which are as wind' (Job

113

6:26). I'm glad that God didn't take what I said seriously.

But all the time, I knew about pain and sanctification. The truth was there, waiting quietly for me to attend to it. Although I raged and whimpered, deep down I knew. I knew that I was being sanctified, and that immeasurable happiness awaits the holy. 'For His anger is but for a moment, His favor is for life; weeping may endure for a night, but joy comes in the morning' (Ps 30:5).

What can I do?

Some things can be changed, so we change them. If this pain could be taken away, you would not hesitate. But it is here to stay for the time being; you know that. So, what can you do?

If you must swim in a river, it is easier to swim with the current. If you must fall, it will hurt much less if you are relaxed. Since we must be sanctified through suffering, it is better to co-operate.

This is a good time for sanctification. For one thing, it seems as if your whole world has fallen apart, therefore it will have to be rebuilt, and this is rather like renovating a building that has been gutted by fire. You *could* restore it to its original state, but it is just as easy to make a few changes. 'I was never quite happy with the staircase the way it was,' says the renovator. Well, God was not very happy with some of the things in us, and now is a good time to make the changes.

Another thing: pleasures are not very pleasurable at the moment. Nothing satisfies. This won't last for ever, so take advantage of it while it lasts. It is pleasures which often draw us from whole-hearted enjoyment of God, so now that they have lost their glory, it is a good

114

time to look closely at our lives. We might see something now which we would not usually let ourselves see.

In addition, you are already racked with questions about whose fault all this is, and however destructive the questions are, they have a beneficial side. You are open to the idea that you might be very much at fault. This is good for your sanctification. If you can ignore the destructive wave of guilt and worthlessness – and that's not easy – then perhaps you can look at the Bible. If you see in the Bible something wrong with yourself, you will probably take it to heart.

'For if anyone is a hearer of the word and not a doer, he is like a man observing his natural face in a mirror; for he observes himself, goes away, and immediately forgets what kind of man he was' (Jas 1:23–24). You are no longer this sort of person, are you? You are prepared to see awful truths (and untruths) about yourself without looking away.

So, flow with the current and make sanctification your priority. I have grown more in holiness through suffering than at any other time, and sudden singleness was no exception. Open your Bible; sink to your knees; seek God in the church; believe, obey.

'Search me, O God, and know my heart; try me, and know my anxieties; and see if there is any wicked way in me, and lead me in the way everlasting' (Ps 139:23–24).

8

Will I Ever Be Happy Again?

It does seem impossible that we will ever be happy again. We may as well ask: 'Will a man walk again if his legs have been amputated? Will he see if his eyes are gone, or hear if he has no ear-drums?'

It isn't as though you wanted to wallow in self-pity – you have refused that temptation. And yes, you do expect the pain to lessen because all pains grow less eventually. What is sick can be healed; what is broken can be mended. But this is different. Something unique, irreplaceable, has gone. If your childhood home burns down, it can never be rebuilt. A new house can be built, but it isn't the same. Similarly, there are artificial limbs, but nothing replaces your own legs.

No one can turn back the clock. Once you were young; once you loved. How fully you trusted then! You cannot imagine trusting again; not so wholeheartedly, at least. And the intensity of first love! Could you love like that again? Your youth has been spent; now you are older. Could you ever be that bright happy person you once were? It seems that the best has been used up.

How can the fear of being hurt – betrayed – again ever go away? And won't this fear remaining at the back of your mind for ever be a shadow over future happiness?

What if it wasn't you who was hurt? You've heard of awful things happening to children at the hands of step-parents.

Happiness, then, seems to be a thing of the past. Or so you think. But you are wrong.

'I am the resurrection'

Never underestimate the power of God. 'Ah, Lord God! Behold, You have made the heavens and the earth by Your great power and outstretched arm. There is nothing too hard for You' (Jer 32:17). Take the case of Lazarus, who was Jesus' friend. When Jesus told a parable of a man who went to heaven, he used Lazarus' name for that man (Lk 16:20). That is how much Jesus thought of him.

Then Lazarus became ill, and they asked Jesus to go and see him. They knew Jesus could heal him. Unaccountably, Jesus delayed, and soon it was 'too late'. 'If You had been here,' said Martha, 'my brother would not have died' (Jn 11:21). *If only!* Now surely it must be too late.

But Martha knew better than that. 'But even now I know that whatever You ask of God, God will give You.' *Even now!* Martha knew it wasn't too late. God can heal someone, even after they are dead and buried. And when he does, he reveals his glory in a special way: 'And I am glad for your sakes,' said Jesus, 'that I was not there, that you may believe' (v.15).

They watched in amazement as the dead man walked out of the tomb.

When all human hope is lost, then God acts in astonishing fashion.

Job had watched in horror as disaster piled upon

disaster. It seemed that things couldn't get any worse, yet they did. His only hope came to lie in death. 'Why did I not die at birth? Why did I not perish when I came from the womb?' (Job 3:11). Since he couldn't take his own life, all that was left was to hope for death. Certainly restoration was hopeless now.

But God acted in this most hopeless time, and he acted as never before. When it happened, Job was dumbfounded. 'I know that You can do everything,' said Job in amazement (42:2). He realised that he hardly knew God – not as he now knew him (42:5). The Spirit emphasised how complete Job's restoration was with: 'Indeed the Lord gave Job twice as much as he had before' (42:10).

The point is, God is the same today.

Job was far better off afterwards than before – in every way. Already a good man, he knew God far better. And what he had lost in earthly things was doubly restored.

Walking towards the light

So you have hope – hope for this life as well as the life to come. You don't know when; you don't know what, but you do know who. It is God, for whom nothing is too hard. He loves you, and has something planned. You may have no better idea than Job what is coming, but remember this: when God plans something special for his children, it is worth waiting for.

So think of it as a light at the end of the tunnel. It is very dark in the tunnel, and the distant light illuminates nothing around you, but it does tell you that the darkness is not for ever. Soon you will be out in the clear light of day. Out there it is warm and sunny. You just need to keep going; keep travelling towards that light. However cold and dark it is now, you will come out into the brightness of day.

'Who walks in darkness and has no light? Let him trust in the name of the Lord and rely upon his God' (Is 50:10). But how do we walk while the darkness is still upon us?

Looking on the good side

Looking on the good side is an art. Or maybe it's a science. There must be a good side to everything for the Christian. There has to be because 'we know that all things work together for good to those who love God, to those who are the called according to His purpose' (Rom 8:28).

'Well,' you will say, 'what's the good side of having no money? Or not seeing the children? Or being lonely?' It isn't easy to answer this. As I said, it's an art – or maybe a science. If you haven't learned the art, or mastered the science, it's high time you did. You will need it more than ever in the days to come.

Here are a few ways that I have used.

The good side of loneliness

If it really were utter loneliness, there wouldn't be a good side. But it isn't because God is real. Being with him is not being alone. People who don't like being with God shouldn't ask to go to heaven – they wouldn't like it there.

'But I could be with God before; this is nothing new,' you say. Of course you could, but it will be much better now.

Being close to God involves faith, as well as repentance, humility and much else. But it also involves

119

seeking him: 'You will seek Me and find Me, when you search for Me with all your heart' (Jer 29:13). Seeking God is more than just an attitude; it is an action. It involves time. We need to spend time praying, praising and listening to God's word.

Alongside your recent losses there is a gain. You now have more time during the quiet moments of the day: first thing in the morning and last thing at night. This is a precious commodity. 'He who is unmarried cares for the things of the Lord – how he may please the Lord. But he who is married cares about the things of the world – how he may please his wife' (1 Cor 7:32–33).

Now, when the day is finished, you go off to bed alone. But you are not alone. Perhaps the day has been busy with the challenges, the victories and the disappointments that make up life. You begin to talk about them – and Somebody is listening. But you've had enough of your own thoughts – you want to hear from someone else – so you open your Bible. 'Speak to me please, Lord,' you murmur as you start to read. You know you are not alone.

Perhaps you're talking to him about your loneliness. And he is listening. What you don't realise is that your friendship with him is deepening all the time – and faster than before. He is getting time that used to go to someone else. You seek him like never before, and you find him like never before.

Loving God seems to loom larger for you now. You're making an effort to see what he wants changed in your life. One thing is clear: there can be no contention between you and God. You surrender to him in a new way. 'Have your way, Lord,' you plead. And, increasingly, he does. This gives you considerable satisfaction. You're glad, too, about how he seems closer to you than before.

It's still painful to be 'alone', but there is a new joy too. God is your joy in a way he wasn't before. Something very good has come out of something very bad. The loss is earthly; the gain is heavenly.

The good side of need

So much is suddenly different. Perhaps you are short of money now, or perhaps you are wondering how you will look after the children alone. Maybe the children are gone, and you miss them and wonder how they will get on. You have so many new needs. It may seem that the one who has gone is all right; they have what they want.

There is an old joke: 'There's one thing that money can't buy – poverty!' But actually there are things that we can't have until we are poor enough; until our needs are great enough. Faith is one of these things.

Ask yourself this: Am I relying on God more now? Am I praying more, asking for more help? They may not seem very polished, but those desperate cries for rescue are prayers.

Needs throw us onto God, and this is a good thing. Abraham learned to trust when he really needed something – he needed an heir – and the process of trusting, and then eventually receiving, was good. It was better than having never been in need, because through asking and trusting and receiving, Abraham was brought closer to God. Eventually, he 'was called the friend of God' (Jas 2:23).

Abraham spent many long years waiting for what he wanted. No doubt others – who were blessed with children in the normal way – found him an amusing figure. 'Abraham' means 'father of a great crowd', so imagine adopting the name 'Abraham' (his name was 'Abram' originally) when you are childless! No doubt it often seemed hard to Abraham, but he had the last laugh when the miracle child came at last, and they named him Isaac (which means 'he laughs').

Abraham is probably laughing still. Two major races – the Jews and the Arabs – trace their lineage back to Abraham, and countless million Christians are his spiritual children. But, best of all, he was God's special friend.

The times when my friendship with God has grown most are the 'bad' times. I never realised, at the time, what I was gaining, but looking back, it was all worthwhile.

But you don't have to wait until you can look back. See the good side of it now.

Living a moment at a time

Perhaps these constant references to time simply horrify you; you cannot comprehend that some time in the future you'll see the good of it all. Perhaps you can't face the future; perhaps you can't even face today.

'Therefore do not worry about tomorrow,' Jesus says, 'for tomorrow will worry about its own things. Sufficient for the day is its own trouble' (Mt 6:34). The challenge is to live today – and survive it. Perhaps it's not even today, but the next few hours, or minutes. If you can live through this moment, and the next, then that is enough. The endless vista of the future is simply a collection of such moments. Let it take care of itself.

But how will you survive the coming moment? 'Put on the Lord Jesus Christ, and make no provision for the flesh, to fulfil its lusts' (Rom 13:14). Get dressed every morning with Jesus. Put him on, like clothes, as the Bible says. Pray that his qualities and reactions will operate, not yours. And don't doubt him. We pray to a God who 'is able to do exceedingly abundantly above all that we ask or think' (Eph 3:20).

He is able to do more than we think because he is at work, even while we feel nothing. Your feelings are likely to be very uneven at the moment, and even if they weren't, they are only the tip of the iceberg. We feel God with us, but he is with us far more than we feel.

Moment by moment, be clothed with him. Ask him to keep you safe, to protect you. Pray that you won't be bitter, and that you'll see the good side. Perhaps you feel something, but perhaps you don't. Trust him anyway. Live as if he is answering your prayers. That is faith, and now you know more about it than if you had never suffered.

Remarriage?

Could you ever trust anyone again? Wouldn't remarriage feel like putting your hand into the trap again? On the other hand, do you yearn to be loved, cherished? What does God say of remarriage?

In Bible terms, you are now a 'widow(er)'. There is no Bible word for someone who has had to divorce an unfaithful partner. God's law punished adultery with death, so the innocent party would become a widow anyway. A divorced person is, in the Bible, 'an unfaithful partner who has been divorced' – assuming the divorce was righteous. 'Widow' is therefore the closest word, although not exactly the same as 'suddenly single'.

What does God say about 'widows'? 'But I say to the unmarried and to the widows: It is good for them if they remain even as I am; but if they cannot exercise self-control, let them marry. For it is better to marry than to burn with passion' (1 Cor 7:8–9). The single life is the highest, according to the Bible, but Paul calls it 'a gift' in verse 7, and not all have it. 'Burning with passion' is a sign that one doesn't have the gift – at least not yet. To those who burn, marriage is recommended.

Nothing in the Bible prohibits remarriage for the innocent party. They are like the single person and the genuine widow. The glories of the single life are offered, but (re)marriage is honourable as well.

The rebound?

But remarriage is fraught with dangers too. Many have married on the rebound soon after sudden singlehood, and the new marriage has ended in disaster. What does God say about the rebound?

The basic Bible principle is: 'Therefore a man shall leave his father and mother and be joined to his wife, and they shall become one flesh' (Gen 2:24). Before he can 'be joined', he must 'leave'. It says that we should leave our parents, because it assumes that we are living with them until we marry. If it is a remarriage, we must have 'left' the previous partner. Surely this creates no problem for you since you were the one who was 'left' anyway! Not so.

The departed partner can be very much present still. Maybe you still love the one who has gone. Perhaps you are looking for someone to replace them. You cannot be 'joined' properly to your new partner if you are really looking for someone else in them.

What if you don't love the one who has gone any more; your love for them has died? They may still be with you, however – very much with you – in your bitter

124

thoughts of them. You haven't left them if they are still in your thoughts. You don't value your new partner for who they are, but because they're not like the one who left. Perhaps your new marriage is even an attempt to prove something to the one who left you.

To avoid the rebound, you must be sure that you have 'left' the one who left you. If you fall in love again, it is as a single person with no ties – good or bad – to anyone else.

A sad second best?

But isn't there something second best about a remarriage? Not necessarily. The things that really matter are love, kindness, humility and gentleness. You will probably have more of these to give than before. You have suffered; that will make you more patient and understanding.

Being deeply and passionately in love is not limited to the young. Jacob was halfway through his long life when he met Rachel: 'So Jacob served seven years for Rachel, and they seemed only a few days to him because of the love he had for her' (Gen 29:20). Only a powerful and passionate love can make seven years of hard work feel like 'a few days'.

So, coming back to our question at the beginning of the chapter: Will I ever be happy again?

Yes. Like you, I have known the deepest, most bitter anguish. I have lived through pain that was greater than I had believed possible. I have known devastation. But not for ever.

I couldn't imagine ever being happy again, but I was wrong. The sorrow ended; its good effects remain.

Sometimes now I am so happy that I want to cry. I want to thank God; I *do* thank God. I tell him that he is wonderful beyond words.

I look back on the miseries, and I thank God that I have suffered only a tiny fraction of what I deserve. His grace has covered my many sins and I can only thank him over and over again.

Sometimes I can hardly believe how God has freed me. But I believe that he used the 'truth to set me free' (Jn 8:32), and I offer this book to you in his name, to witness to that truth. These Bible truths – imperfectly understood and explained by me – will be used by God to free you too. As you trust him, the sorrows and anguish will pass away. You will be speechless with joy.

> I love the Lord, because He has heard my voice and my supplications. Because He has inclined His ear to me, therefore I will call upon Him as long as I live. The pains of death surrounded me, and the pangs of Sheol laid hold of me; I found trouble and sorrow. Then I called upon the name of the Lord: 'O Lord, I implore You, deliver my soul!' Gracious is the Lord, and righteous; yes, our God is merciful. The Lord preserves the simple; I was brought low, and He saved me. Return to your rest, O my soul, for the Lord has dealt bountifully with you. For You have delivered my soul from death, my eyes from tears, and my feet from falling. I will walk before the Lord in the land of the living (Ps 116:1–9).